More praise for
HOW TO LIVE IN THE WORLD
AND STILL BE HAPPY

"Hugh Prather's gentle spirit and infinite wisdom give us the tools and insight to see what happiness really means and where it resonates. In these times of spiritual awakening, this book serves as a beacon lighting the path to happiness."

—JACKIE WALDMAN, author of
Teachers with the Courage to Give and *Teens with the Courage to Give*

"*How to Live in the World and Still Be Happy* gives focus to things we often forget: we each have power and we each have choice."

—IYANLA VANZANT, author of
Yesterday I Cried and *One Day My Soul Just Opened Up*

"Prather writes what he lives. By totally accepting his own humanity, he knows happiness."

—CHANDRA ALEXANDER, author of *Reality Works*

"A balm to the soul, *How to Live in the World and Still Be Happy* is an invaluable map for our journey toward peace of mind and happiness."

—SUE PATTON THOELE, author of
The Courage to Be Yourself and *The Woman's Book of Confidence*

How To Live in the World and Still Be Happy

HUGH PRATHER

CONARI PRESS

A version of this material was previously published as *Notes on How to Live in the World and Still Be Happy*.

ISBN: 1-57324-818-5

Cover and book design: Suzanne Albertson
Author photo: John C. Prather

Library of Congress Cataloging-in-Publication Data

Prather, Hugh.
    How to live in the world and still be happy / Hugh Prather.
        p.   cm.
    Rev. ed. of: Notes on how to live in the world—and still be happy.
    ISBN 1-57324-818-5
        1. Conduct of life. 2. Happiness. I. Prather, Hugh. Notes on how to
        live in the world—and still be happy. II. Title.
    BJ1581.2 .P74 2002
    158.1–dc21   2002010384

Printed in Canada.

02 03 04 05 TCP 10 9 8 7 6 5 4 3 2 1

Fortunately, this book has been equally
Gayle's in the making and, together,
we dedicate it to Bill Thetford.

How to Live in the World and Still Be Happy

UNHAPPINESS

Love of Misery

Happiness is easy. It's letting go of unhappiness that's hard. We are willing to give up everything but our misery.

Clearly, we are all a little crazy. Yet to favor unhappiness over happiness may seem sane at first glance. Right now, the world is not an easy place to live, and it never really has been. So why should we think we can live in it happily? Or that we would even want to?

Take for example the things we desire. The irony is, if you want it, it's usually not good for you, and if you pursue it, it will hurt you. But who can help wanting and pursuing? And just look at the unhappy results. It doesn't matter whether the object of our desire is large or small, whether it is wealth, eminence, influence, or merely the juiciest gossip, the tastiest foods, the most erotic pleasures: The outcome is some degree of misery. We dismiss this as the "the downside," but our fear of "side effects" and "fallout" weighs more heavily on our minds than perhaps we like to admit.

Surely the answer must lie in simple hard work. The key is to be a plodder who wishes little and seeks slowly. But even the plodder runs into one of life's ironies. The fruits of our labor, whatever slice of life they represent and however patiently earned, will be taken from us in the end. Lifetime after lifetime, the story is retold of eventual loss, loneliness, and painful death. We will see everyone we know die, or they will see us die. Our loved ones may be in the room when our life ends, but they can't die for us. Can anyone realistically escape how the story ends? And knowing well the outcome, how can anyone expect to live happily and at peace?

So perhaps the potential for happiness is in the many years leading up to death—all the good times that outweigh how our life will end.

No matter what our age, nothing we see in the world is wholly reliable. Even the preschool playground is a place where someone is your best friend today but tomorrow wants only to play with some other child. There is no place where we cannot wear out our welcome. Parents turn away from their children in a thousand ways, and when children grow up, they turn from their parents. In all walks of life, in every form of life, the strong prey upon the weak until they in turn are weak and are preyed upon. The world contains much physical beauty, yet everything lives off the death of something else. This is certainly not all there need be to our experience, but despite the few scattered exceptions, for these and countless other reasons the world is a very difficult place to live.

But is that difficulty a sufficient reason not to be happy? It would certainly appear so. And despite all the forms that misery takes, if there really were a way to live happily, wouldn't it be immoral, insensitive, or inhumane to choose that way for ourselves?

Is it moral to be happy when a quarter or more of the people on the Earth are starving? When a third or more of the nations are engaged in armed conflict? When the numbers of those who can cause nuclear catastrophe or some other form of global devastation are growing inexorably? And what of pollution, discrimination, endangered species, detention and torture, plagues and degenerative illnesses, the signs of pending geological cataclysm, and the worldwide increase in violence and terrorism? What our mood should be is . . .

Angry? Shocked? Sad? Outraged? Depressed?

And instead of applying ourselves to becoming happier, what we should be spending our time doing is . . .

Identifying and bringing to light the people who are causing all of this?

Working to defeat candidates who disagree with us?

Taking steps to protect our personal supplies of food, money, and shelter?

Giving away what we have to the needy?

Marching? Writing e-mails?

Giving speeches? Holding prayer vigils?

Fear of Happiness

These are indeed bitter questions. And few have agreed on an answer. Obviously there is no widespread consensus, and it's equally obvious there never has been. Nor is it the purpose of this book to make another futile attempt to rally support for still one more unworkable solution. It should be clear that there is entrenched guilt over lightheartedness and substantial fear that when we take time out to be happy we are not protecting our interests, and certainly not doing all we could for the world.

Although for many it's perhaps unconscious, we carry with us the sabotaging belief that we don't deserve to be happy. To have any aspect of our lives run more smoothly than is "natural" is somehow proof of our guilt. Whenever things are going "too" well, we fear some vague, undefined retribution, as if the world has a consciousness that keeps track of these things, and since we are not getting our quota of hardship, the balance soon will be set right.

The news and entertainment media contribute to this attitude. It is very difficult to sit in front of the TV night after night and not come to believe that tragedy is to be expected in every life and that some form of natural law is being violated if this is not presently true for us.

From radio, newspapers, TV, and the Internet; from cause-oriented movies, books, and magazines; from scare letters on behalf of every conceivable cause; from a constant stream of out-of-town speakers; and from the warnings and admonitions tucked in conversations throughout the day, we get a steady picture of a world ever fretting and wringing its hands. Whether in good times or bad, the ordinary and the prominent all do it. So we assume there must be some value in this time-honored attraction to misery.

Thus we have come to believe that we must keep our guard up at all times. We also believe that if we are happy, we have let our guard down. This means our minds must stay focused on all the dark corners. We must never allow ourselves to forget a single painful experience. And we must persistently catalog every upcoming event that could turn against us. Yet have you noticed how much of what we think will happen never does?

Just consider for a moment the countless hours most of us spend fantasizing our reactions to things that will never be, formulating answers to remarks we will never hear. And if for a moment we run out of future twists of fate to imagine, we go back in time and rewrite events and conversations that have long since ended. It is sad to realize how we could use our minds instead. If some step can be taken in the present that will make us or our loved ones feel safer, then let us by all means take it. But that of course is not what we are speaking of here.

The world is indeed a dangerous place, and obviously there are times when the worst we fear does happen. Yet what did being sick with dread ever do to protect us? Fear neither causes the thing feared to happen nor prevents it. It is mere static. It is an absence of music. It is not power. There is calmness at the center of us, a very deep well of happiness that cannot be exhausted, but it will never be experienced while our perceptions are twisted by doubt and fear.

A thousand times a day our love of happiness is cut short by our even greater fear of it. Even a little cheerfulness is checked if it goes on too long. If we find ourselves laughing with complete freedom, singing in the shower, or maybe just whistling loud enough to be overheard, the old anxiety begins seeping in. Our "frivolous" mood is being called into question. For some nagging reason we must resume a "serious" state of mind, although just why this is helpful or proper we are not quite sure.

Happiness is serious. It is very serious, not only as it affects our health, job, children, and all other aspects of our life, but also in how it influences, perhaps even changes, the world. I am obviously not in a position to know the effect each individual's state of mind has on the whole, but it seems clear that we have a mental influence that extends beyond our words and physical gestures.

This influence is usually given negative credit. People talk of the "vibe" being bad in a certain building or the aura being bad around a certain person. But of course it should go both ways, and I believe it does. We are either throwing our mental weight into the balance of fear and hate, or we are adding to the world's measure of hope and kindness. This cannot be seen of course, but it is most certainly experienced. If we need justification for being happy, we might ask, What is the alternative?

What do we believe the various forms of unhappiness can do to relieve the world's misery?

Surely we will not lessen anguish by maintaining the very state of mind we wish to see the other members of our worldly family released from. No matter what our words or actions, to be bitter, cynical, or offended is to teach our faith in the value of these emotions.

It is curious how often peace is championed unpeacefully, and how often in the name of a broader kindness we feel justified in being unkind to a few people. Okay to snipe and lash out or to be insensitive and selfish, provided the cause is grand. We even think it's logical to attack our children in order to teach them not to attack, to scold them into being more respectful. But a temporary change in outward behavior is all we get, for doesn't our *mood* teach what we really believe the most effective approach to life is?

I believe that to be consistently harmless is to bolster this urge within the mental atmosphere of the world—even if in small measure. And I believe that a little gain is better than none.

Who really knows the effect of one happy thought? Is it possible that it circles the globe, finding entry into any open heart, encouraging and giving hope in some unseen way? I am convinced it does. For whenever I am truly loving, I feel the warmth and presence of the like-minded, a growing family whose strength lies in their gentleness and whose message is in their treatment of others. I believe it is good and right to be happy, and I know from experience that it is the only way I personally can be kind.

HAPPINESS

Can Happiness Last?

The belief that there is no permanent happiness is so widespread and deeply rooted that it's simply a hard fact of life for most people. Should some holy foreign visitor claim—or even appear—otherwise, he or she either is not believed or is thought to be a fake or a phenomenon. And why not? Who has experienced even one day of "perfect peace"? A whole life of it seems preposterous.

We've heard it said that individuals in their right mind would not *want* consistent happiness. Which raises an interesting question. Is it possible *not* to want what by definition one wants?

The Merriam-Webster unabridged has this to say about the durability of happiness: "A state of well-being characterized by relative permanence . . . and by a natural desire for its continuation." The Oxford English definition includes this indication of *where* happiness occurs: "The state of pleasurable content of mind. . . ."

Dictionaries merely report how a word is commonly used, and true to general usage, all the ones I've looked at cite good luck, prosperity, and other forms of worldly success as the principle origins of happiness. This is not only how the word is used but also the general belief in how this "content of mind" comes and goes. It is a "beautiful feeling" that we want to endure, but it is dependent on how outward events go. "Oh, what a beautiful morning. Oh, what beautiful day... Everything's going my way."

But for how long do things go our way? We want a better wardrobe. But for how long will it be better? We want a better salary. But for how long will it be better? And so it is with couch, car, or complexion. Nothing remains the best; nothing remains even better—whether lover, lawn, or laptop. Is it any wonder, then, that we don't believe in lasting happiness, even though we have "a natural desire for its continuation"? The way we have happiness set up in our minds, it's a decidedly unhappy subject. For the sake of our own happiness, we had best forget it altogether as a rational goal. That is, unless we can find another source besides "Everything's going my way."

Is it possible to say, "Nothing has to go right today" and still be happy? In fact, it's the only way.

Because nothing will go right, as I'm sure you've noticed by now. It started again this morning. A little something spills, certain people are late as usual, our hair is never quite right, and then there's the neighbor's dog. Forget hate and greed—is there any real hope of eliminating all annoying noises, smells, poor workmanship, overpriced products, traffic gridlock, and rudeness in stores? Then why get so caught up in the very nature of the day that simple enjoyment becomes impossible? As the song says, "You can't roller-skate in a buffalo herd, but you can be happy if you've a mind to." The key is "having a mind to."

The Grounds for Happiness

There is a mental state that passes gently and easily over the endless nonsense that litters the day. Like a soft breeze, it refreshes everything but disturbs nothing. It's happy just being itself. And being something, it has something to give. Its opposite is the mental state that is constantly getting entangled and pulled down by almost everything. Unhappiness is unfocused, agitated, and above all, scared. Having no integrity, no calm inner direction, it takes its cue from whatever problem is perceived to be before it now.

The mind *can* be trained, yet in most instances our thoughts are so chaotic and vulnerable that we go through the day looking at everyone through a thick mental haze that blocks from view what each person is at heart. Yet it is seeing the urges of the heart that makes us happy. Babies and very young children, for example, make us happy because we allow ourselves to see their basic innocence. In their case we are quick to see *because* we are slow to judge.

Although it's by no means inevitable, the ordinary efforts made during the passing of years can occasionally bring about a small measure of the mental wholeness needed to permit a gentler vision. That is why older parents, and especially grandparents, often enjoy children more than do "the young and the restless." By the time we reach middle age, we have sometimes learned enough to devote ourselves to our children and not just squeeze them in among a bewildering array of conflicting pursuits.

Children, like everything else of value, cannot be hurried. The pleasure that a baby or young child has to offer is as delicate and subtle as a sunrise. Sitting quietly in the hush of dawn, with nothing to do and nowhere to go, we hear the waking sounds of the Earth and see the shifts in light and shadow that a more hurried mind will miss. Haste makes unhappiness. The happiness within us is very still. It is not physically slow; it is merely at peace.

It is silly to hold children up as models of behavior. They obviously don't come into the world equipped with everything they need to remain happy, or else they would remain so. But children do start with certain strengths, especially mental strength, that many of us have lost. A child can prove that it is possible to be extremely active and interested in everything and still be happy, provided that a uniting goal dominates the mind.

Gayle and I were asked to bring our son John to the first wedding we conducted, not only to the service itself (during which he comported himself reasonably well for someone who had been alive for only two years) but also to the formal wedding dinner that followed. The meal was to be at a "nice" restaurant, and I asked the couple if they knew what they were letting themselves in for. "Oh yes!" they laughed. Even though Gayle and I know it is best to take children only where they can be their age, the wedding party were unusually child-tolerant folk. So we decided to make an exception.

The table was formally set, with a rolled white linen napkin inside each empty water glass. As a boy I had learned that at nice restaurants, unless one is eating bouillabaisse, one does not tuck one's napkin into one's collar, and in the case of bouillabaisse, one titters guiltily as the waiter applies the bib. But somehow I had missed the one about the proper moment to put the napkin in your lap. With an ancient fear I looked at it elevated before me. Any mistake now would be highly visible.

John pulled out his napkin, played tent for a few seconds, then put all his utensils into the glass.

I started to speak to him, but looking around and seeing no consternation, I held off.

He took out an imaginary box of matches and began "lighting" each fork, spoon, and knife. He explained to the whole table that this was a birthday cake and they were going to blow out the candles. As the glass was passed around, he watched carefully for omissions and patiently pointed out such things as, "You missed the spoon," and made the person blow again.

All this was taken in great spirits, and so I began to relax a little and just watch.

The first course served was salad. It came garnished with olives. I knew John didn't like olives, but whereas not liking an ingredient could ruin a dish for me, John saw that these sliced black olives were actually racing tires, and within seconds he had set up a drag strip on his bread plate. The right combination of black olives and white porcelain can simulate "laying down rubber" with remarkable resemblance.

I will not go through the entire dinner in which the grated cheese became modeling clay, and so forth. Obviously John was operating within an exceptional atmosphere. Plus the fact that all young children know they have you at their mercy in a place where you don't want to make a scene.

Children, if they are to interact happily, must eventually learn that most adults have strong opinions about how water glasses, napkins, black olives, and everything else in the world should be used. It will not make a child happy to buck this. We once took a neighbor's four-year-old girl to a magic show, and the woman who had the seat next to her scolded her for squirming excitedly. "Little girl," she said loudly, "you are disturbing me!" Of course it was her own unquestioned outlook about how everything should be that was disturbing her.

But it's pointless to fight these things. We simply told little Melissa to sit still, even though half the audience was composed of excited, squirming children. That was all that was necessary. To have done more than was necessary—for example, to have snapped at the woman—would have made everyone concerned unhappy and would not have pushed the woman in a happier direction.

It is their single vision, so free of the past, that children have to teach, not the particular way they act it out. Adults are not required to play tent with their napkins in order to acquire strength of purpose. Even children themselves express single-mindedness in different ways. A five-year-old might like to use fingers to make shadow figures on the wall, whereas a five-month-old will like trying to grab fingers as they move. Yet both are certain there is a way to enjoy fingers. Children are so noticeably decisive because they have made a single decision about everything. John, as almost any small child would have done, saw it all—the table setting, the people, the food—through the lens of a single interpretation. Everything was there to be enjoyed, and he was positive it could be.

It is evident that the opposite occurs as we "mature." Each thing in the world begins taking on a separate and restricted function. Until that dinner, a linen napkin had only one small purpose for me, and not a very happy one. For most adults this kind of pettiness has already blanketed the world they see. I'm sure you know people who will not cultivate relationships with anyone who wouldn't serve as a step toward money or social advancement. For them, people exist only to use. This is an exceedingly unhappy way of seeing. Whereas in the eyes of the very young, even an individual's physical deformity can be a thing of great interest, or of no particular interest, but not a reason for uneasiness and discomfort. Naturally, as kids get older and pick up more adult values, they can be quite cruel about the same deformities.

Years ago I watched some four-year-olds go into a pool that normally contained preschoolers but on this day contained only adults with Down syndrome. These four-year-olds had never seen an individual with Down syndrome. In watching them play, and afterward in listening to their chatter, I realized they had not seen one that day either. Since children are so observant, it's probably more accurate to say they found the differences between themselves and the others in the pool too unimportant to react to or even comment on. The adults were having great fun, and to the children that was what counted.

Thinking Coats the World

"There is nothing either good or bad, but thinking makes it so." Shakespeare has Hamlet say these words in an exchange with Rosencrantz in which the latter points out that Hamlet would not think of his country and the world as a prison if he were not ambitious.

It's fortunate that our thinking gives things the meaning they have for us, because we have very little control over things. Yet we have complete control over thinking, at least potentially. However, it doesn't follow that in order to be surrounded by good things, we must fill our minds with "good thoughts." Telling ourselves that everyone is good at heart and every occurrence is a blessing is a sure way to inner turmoil. Because it runs up hard against our basic honesty.

Thinking *makes* it so. Thinking coats the world. The world has surprisingly little effect on our happiness until it's coated and given meaning by us. When Jordan was six months old he liked sitting up better than lying back in his portable carrier, so we began putting him in a walker, even though his legs were not yet strong enough to move it. One day Gayle had just gone into the kitchen when a friend came in the front door. They both heard a crashing noise from the bathroom. They went to investigate and found Jordan flat on his back, staring curiously up from the bottom of a full bathtub.

It seems Jordan had picked that exact moment to begin

"walking." The bathroom had a sunken tub and he had fallen in. Needless to say, they were horrified at seeing a baby staring up at them under two feet of water. They pulled him out, started drying him off, and yelled for me to come.

I ran in and they explained what had happened. We all stood there waiting for Jordan (who was soon dry and freshly diapered) to start crying. But he never did. In fact, when we set him back in the walker, he headed for the tub as fast as he could, and we immediately had to put up a barrier to the bathroom.

There was nothing in this six-month-old boy's thinking to tell him that lying under warm water when you can't swim is "bad." Evidently the memory of his recent womb experience told him that the sensation was "good."

Thoughts Connect or Separate

We've all heard the expressions "That's a comforting thought" and "That's a disturbing thought." A neighbor once said something similar that gave me insight into one way I disturb other people. Although his work was psychiatry, his passion was new cameras of every size and make. His wife and children were very patient with him about this, and whenever he made one of his frequent purchases, they always smiled and seemed sincerely pleased for him. One day we were visiting and once again Bill brought out a new camera to show us. After admiring it and asking pertinent questions, I laughed and said, "How many cameras do you have now, Bill?"

He seemed subdued for a second or two, then replied, "That's not a happy question." And indeed, as is so often true of kidding, it was not.

These expressions—"That's a comforting thought," "That's a disturbing thought," "There is nothing either good or bad, but thinking makes it so"—acknowledge the same fact. Once thought, an idea is part of our perception. In a sense it becomes the eyes through which we see. It determines what we pick out to notice and what we choose to overlook. The thought itself, and not its object, comforts and makes happy, giving support, hope, or self-confidence. Just as the thought, and not the subject of the thought, takes comfort and strength away. More important, our thoughts lead to connection or to separation. We experience ourselves as alone or as part of something greater than ourselves, depending on which thoughts we use to view the world.

Yet this is a difficult insight for most people to practice. We aren't in the habit of looking at just thought alone. There is a profound tendency to confuse what we see with how we are looking. Nevertheless, it is indispensable to our happiness that we appreciate the difference. "How many cameras do you have now?" is not a "bad" subject. Another person might have liked toting them up. The unhappiness was in the intent of a question that concealed a mild judgment, but a judgment nonetheless.

Anger Is Never Discrete

Good will and ill will are entire mindsets. Anger originates in the mind and infects the entire mind with which we think. There are no confined attacks. Whenever we condemn, we cloak the world with pain. When we love, we bless indiscriminately.

Several years ago Gayle and I were able to do little more than stand by and watch as the only child of a couple we knew grew sicker and weaker from a congenital defect. The doctors had tried everything. Now the couple could devote themselves only to loving their son and making him happy and comfortable, which they did exceedingly well and with all their hearts. Finally, just before his fourth birthday, the boy died.

This couple had unusual strength and resiliency. Their grief was enormous, yet their focus quickly began to shift away from their personal sorrow to helping other parents who might be working through the same shock and loss. At that time there were no groups in Santa Fe to which people in grief could turn, so the four of us decided to start one. We put a notice in the paper, contacted hospitals and churches, and held our first meeting in a small conference room of the branch library.

All four of us knew that this was going to be a fundamentally grim and depressing activity. But we were wrong. As the sessions continued, we were surprised to find that although there was silence and crying and deep outpourings of emotion, on the whole these weekly meetings were remarkably happy and uplifting. I can remember on more than one occasion when people coming for the first time would stick their heads in the door and we quickly had to assure them that despite all the laughter, they had indeed found the "grief support group."

Gayle and I observed several dynamics in these meetings that helped us better understand happiness. One in particular kept repeating with almost every new member. When individuals forgave totally, letting go of all grudges and bitterness, their grief began dissipating dramatically. But as long as some deep anger remained, the grief would persist, sometimes for many years, regardless of what therapeutic measures the person took.

Many of these people had abundant reason to be angry. Their accounts of mistakes made by doctors and nurses or of insensitive remarks by relatives and friends were sometimes so outrageous that the group would be left speechless. However, time and again we saw them come to realize that if they truly wanted to be free of grief, the question they had to ask themselves—despite the justification, despite even continued provocation—was how much longer did they want to remain angry over this?

We have no chance of being happy when we are angry. Yet we live in a time when anger is honored as one of the most useful emotions. In a thousand variations we hear the sentiment voiced: "It is self-affirming to be angry." As long as individuals fail to question this assumption, they never discover what it's like to go through one entire day in peace. Something inevitably comes up to justify their irritation. And, naturally, the possibility of day upon day of peace seems hopelessly out of reach.

Because anger never occurs at the deepest level, it can be relinquished without hypocrisy. To see what we really want clears the mind of superficial passions, and even of chronic bitterness. However, without preliminary groundwork, most people do not reach a place where they can quickly see their true feelings. For them, the question is what must they do to make this possible.

As a first step, it is far better to remain confused than to lash out. Do not permit the body to act out your desire to attack. Stopping short of involving other people in your distress will save you time. Of course, that alone will not eliminate the surface layer of emotions. With even mild irritation you must turn quickly away from justification and probe the anger itself. Otherwise you will continue to believe it is how you really feel. To look so carefully at the anger that you see through it to your heart is to learn how to use the greatest corrective force there is.

CHAPTER

3

THOUGHTS

"I Feel Good About Myself"

Most of us give lip service to the idea that happiness is a state of mind. Yet we consistently fail to treat it as such. We are afraid that if happiness is mental, we can be personally diminished by this fact. For if it's an inner state, we alone are responsible for our happiness. And no one but us can be blamed for our unhappiness.

All criticism attacks the criticizer. In biblical terms, "If you judge others, you will be judged, and the measure you give will be the measure you receive." It is difficult to accept this ancient insight, which is present in all major religions, because it appears to threaten our worth as a person. We believe that we are thought more highly of when we see to it that someone else is thought less of. If we wish to sustain a feeling of superiority, we must see to it that the people around us feel their inferiority. It is therefore crucial to our self-image that we believe our judgments can leave us and attach themselves to the person who is our target.

It would perhaps be possible to rid ourselves of disparaging thoughts if we were to change our mind about people after condemning them. Yet even this we don't think we can afford, because we also believe we sustain our opinion of ourselves by continuing to criticize. If suddenly we forget to condemn and instead recognize the other person's basic innocence, where does this leave us? Indeed that is the question.

For so very long we have not allowed ourselves the smallest doubt that we have been unfairly treated and damaged. We can cite all who are responsible, what they did, and what they should have done instead. If the rules of behavior we have chosen to emphasize are a little easier on us than others, we rectify this by occasionally turning the guns of our disapproval on ourselves. This we call "admitting our faults," and we are careful to do it in the context of someone else's greater fault. In our upside-down way of thinking, it is whom we criticize, and not whether, that matters. Yet in the case of unhappiness, judgmental thoughts are the primary factor. Whether the target is oneself or others, some object or some situation, the result is self-inflicted mental damage.

All thoughts are circular. However much we want to stand apart from our accusations, if we still believe them, they remain an irritant to our mind. Nor is this condition improved by acting out our disapproval. To inform someone of the faults we see does not weaken our belief in them. To the contrary, all that "venting" our judgments produces, aside from a feeling of righteousness and a little bodily numbness, is the enervating sense that the problem is now beyond our control, because we have spread it to other minds and have drawn more egos into our unhappiness.

It's true that by voicing criticism we "get it out," but it is not true that it's any less in because it is now out. If anything, it has been emphasized, hardened, and will stay with us longer. Added to the condemnation is also the sadness that always accompanies betrayal. We have attacked, however mildly, another human being, a person who, just like us, has tried hard.

Obviously nothing being said here applies to people in the news with whom we have no personal relationship, any more than it applies to fictitious characters in a movie or a book. Individuals who cite the monsters of history as deserving condemnation are merely ducking the question of how their state of mind impacts their own loved ones.

It is possible to be open and honest without attacking. It is also possible to beat on a bed, scream into the wind, go for a walk in a nourishing setting, tear up phone books, take a shower, go for a run, or do other physical things that may release bodily tensions and clarify feelings, yet still deal with our emotions within ourselves. This form of "acting out" is harmless because it doesn't complicate the problem by stirring up other people or increasing the numbers involved.

Inner Healing

The rule is, *Don't allow the criticism to leave your mind. Remove its source and repair the damage to your mind quickly.*

This guideline entails no loss. First, until we actually release the disapproval, we only have the illusion that it's not a part of us because it concerns someone else. Second, we do wish to act quickly for the simple reason that the longer we dwell on another's weakness, the more we infect our own mind with this form of unhappiness.

By far the most difficult part of the guideline is "Remove its source." Not because the procedure is complicated, but because our habit of blame is old and deeply rooted. This is especially obvious when "the source" is childhood damage. It isn't possible to reach the kind of happiness we have been speaking of without seeing one's parents as *completely* innocent. There are other blocks to happiness, but this one is universal. Most of us think that because we have renounced our childhood and are not acting the way our parents acted, we have forgiven the past. But of course we haven't.

Gayle and I once watched a friend work very hard, not for just a few minutes or hours but for many months, before she began to make progress in forgiving her father, even though he had been dead for years. By the time she reached forty, she had come to realize that her bitterness over her childhood was so entrenched that, among other manifestations, she would continue to have turbulent, unendurable relationships until she stopped looking at men from the perspective of her past and seeing their every act through the lens of her father's behavior.

She worked out a daily program, the main component of which was to carry a notebook in which she wrote down any symptom of anger (frustration, criticism, irritation, impatience). She chose anger because it was the primary emotion she felt toward her dad. At the end of the day she read her entries and traced each one as far back into her personal history as she could remember. She did this by asking herself, "What does this emotion remind me of most recently? What does it remind me of before that? And before that?" In this way she was able to discern the pattern of behavior that surrounded the history of this emotion.

In our friend's case she saw that as a child she had indeed been a victim of her father, but as an adult it had been her choice to think like a victim. She also noticed that the times in her life she felt most like a victim were also the times she was most destructive.

Another personal effort she made was to ask her dad, who had died eighteen years before, for help. She described the process to us in this way: "I made the leap of faith that my father's spirit is one with God and therefore always present, and I mentally asked for his support whenever I needed a little encouragement. I knew that my goal was as important to him as to me."

She gradually began to feel her dad's gentle, reassuring presence, and she realized that he was no longer the unsupportive, emotionally aggressive figure she remembered. After a good six or seven months of recording anger-related emotions and asking for help, along with experiencing many pleasant changes in her internal atmosphere, she was able, for the first time in her life, to form a new, and this time lasting, relationship.

Most people would not persist as long as did our friend. If the change does not come quickly, our tendency is to dive back into the old way. This woman had come to recognize that as long as she continued to carry a residue of bitterness, as long as there remained even a small persistent grudge, her enjoyment of life would be vulnerable.

Shortly after the new relationship began, she realized that a little of the old anger still remained, and so she immediately went back to work in the same simple way—looking past her surface emotions to what she truly yearned to be and what she believed most deeply was valuable.

Forgiveness

Yesterday Gayle and I walked out of a store, our arms filled with bags of Halloween candy, and opened the back doors of our car. Suddenly I heard an angry voice yell, "Watch it, this is a new Lexus!" Evidently the door I had swung open stopped just short of the side mirror of the car next to us. It had not touched it, but it had come outrageously close, at least in the opinion of the person sitting in the driver's seat, glaring at me. As we drove off, I was surprised at how difficult it was for me to stop thinking about this incident.

Was this a situation that called for forgiveness? Not in the way most people think of forgiveness.

Forgiveness is an often misused, misunderstood, and fearful concept. I wonder if it's even a useful concept for most people. Perhaps tolerance and compassion are more suitable ideas, unless we are trying to deal with an old bitterness or a deep betrayal.

Frequently forgiveness is a type of arrogance. We look down in pity on those who "need" forgiving. Used in this way it is mere attack. We also assume that certain behavior must accompany it. If we forgive someone we don't like, we'll have to spend more time with them. We won't be able to fire an incompetent employee. We'll have to pay whatever alimony our ex demands.

To forgive you need do nothing. It is an act of the heart, not of the body. Genuine forgiveness contains not a hint of the supposed necessity to force the mind to behave, to positively reinterpret what happened, or to reason dishonestly.

To forgive is merely to hand back whatever polluted gift our ego has just handed us. It is to give up a narrow point of view and accept a broader, more relaxed perspective. It is to stop harboring unhappiness. Seen in this way, forgiving is a restful process.

A premise of pure truth lies behind why letting go, or forgiveness, works. The mind is innately happy until made to be otherwise. When the unnatural use of the mind is relinquished, happiness is seen already in place, like the sun "coming out" from behind clouds.

The source of any critical thought must be removed before the damage it has caused to our mind can be repaired. What then is the source? As you can see in the case of our friend, if the source had been external, if it had been her childhood, her dad, or her new boyfriend, her plight would have been bleak indeed. Her childhood was now lost in time and could not be relived except in fantasy; her dad was dead, and her current lover was "wired" however he was wired. Yet all this was irrelevant. Although the damage began in childhood, it was carried on by how she continued to use her mind in the present. And this was within her ability to alter.

When any judgmental train of thought ends, the damage it caused to the mind ends with it. That is precisely why our friend spent so many months quietly looking at the pain her choice for darkness caused herself and others. She wanted to be informed of the dimensions of her bitterness and its harmful effects. She knew that once she saw this clearly, motivation to complete the task of forgiveness would never again be lacking.

We are unable to forgive because we don't want to. It really is that simple. For instance, some parents forgive their adult children of horrific crimes—because they want to. Some husbands and wives forgive their spouse for the gross negligence that killed their child—because they want to. Some mothers and fathers forgive the man who raped their daughter—because they want to. However, far smaller transgressions than these can be quite difficult to forgive. We desperately need the evidence of the other person's guilt. It makes us feel innocent, and in carrying out acts of blame we gain a sense of empowerment and superiority. Yet we no longer have use for any of this once we see what it does to our mind, our health, and our relationships.

"Honesty"

True forgiveness is never dishonest. It is not some futile exercise in rosy self-deception. To the contrary, it is a calm recognition that underneath our egos we are basically the same. Yet we live in a time when the concept of honesty itself is extensively and popularly misused.

The ego part of us—what some call our shadow side, inner demons, or little self—demands loyalty strictly to itself. Even though our tastes and prejudices are never steady and are based on a pitifully narrow point of view, if we are to be righteous within their terms, we must be "honest" or faithful to these feelings. As the expression goes, we must "honor ourself."

In the course of a day, we are likely to be asked what we think of a person's new coat, their new boyfriend or girlfriend, or whether something makes them look fat. Maybe someone tells us a story of how they were mistreated, or they comment on the weather, or just ask, "How's it going?" The ego's ideal of honesty dictates that these conversational snippets be answered from our mood, that we be "honest," even though we may cover our little murders with amenities. In simple truth these overtures are almost never seeking more from us than a little acceptance and appreciation. Since in our hearts we know this, to react to them literally is truly dishonest.

We have a choice. We can consult our intuition and goodwill and respond from love, or we can hand out our current ego opinion and make that our "truthful" answer. There is no mistaking which choice the majority makes and why most people walk away from even the most casual of social contacts feeling a little depressed, anxious, or misunderstood.

Gayle is a far better cook than I am, but we each have dishes that we think we do well. We had been married seventeen years before we realized that time and again we had made each other unhappy by thinking we had to respond "honestly" when asked, "How do you like it?"

"Too dull. It needs some green chilies and a little cumin."

"Yes, but I don't like to over-season everything the way you do. And besides, the children have to eat it."

"So why did you ask me if you didn't want my opinion?"

"I just wanted to know if you thought it had finished baking."

"It depends on how you define 'finished.'"

One night after another one of these pointless exchanges, we sat down and decided that we were going to eliminate this seventeen-year-old bone of contention once and for all. We came up with a rule. Unless it was impossible to keep down, we would always say that the dish was just wonderful, and no matter how closely cross-examined, we would not back down. We expected this plan to eliminate a sore point, but it actually provided a running joke that continues to delight us.

We always have the option of not consulting our ego— unless of course the person really is seeking our ego position. For example, if you are being asked by your partner if you can live happily in this particular house for sale, and you know that you can't, then of course you must say so, for to be a martyr would jeopardize the future peace of your home life.

We frequently choose not to consult our egos when dealing with someone very young. We instinctively know that it's unnecessary to give children our opinion of their first drawings or to critique their innocent attempts at completing a new task. We don't even bother to see what our judgments are. Instead, we speak to the child out of our kindness and happiness. And it's our privilege to do likewise with adults. It is always *possible* to view anything—a new building in town, the lifestyle of certain groups, the climate, the time of day— from our quiet core instead of from our personal history or current disgruntlements.

When John was small he would periodically announce that *he* would do the dishes. He sprayed, soaped, scrubbed, rinsed— he did all the necessary procedures. It's just that he didn't do them in the right order. By the time he finished there were remarkably few clean dishes and a great deal of water everywhere. Yet he was always proud of his job, and we told him how proud we were of him, for truly we were.

It is a part of realism and sanity, and it's certainly a part of happiness, to look upon the world the way we allow ourselves to look at a child. Any child can be seen as annoying, and some adults consistently choose this view. But most of us do not. We see the blamelessness in the eighteen-month-old even though she says "No" to everything. A little baby remains sweet and absolutely pure in our eyes even during a diaper change. If we could but take this gaze and turn it upon the world, we wouldn't have to do one thing more to be constantly and deeply happy.

Our so-called honest way of looking pervades every waking hour and can easily set the tone of an entire lifetime. It's surprising how bitter many people become. Our morning chores, our job, our drive home, our kids, our evening pastimes are either viewed with sympathy and perspective or in the harsh but apparently virtuous light of "honesty." A gentle vision makes a gentler world in which to live.

Mired in the superficial layer of our emotions, we can feel quite certain of the carelessness, selfishness, callousness, or viciousness of another individual. We may in fact have perceived correctly this person's ego characteristics. Yet where does being right take us except into harshness and isolation? Indeed we all have egos. But our own shadow identities are often no better than anyone else's. Even in this we tend to be equal.

Each of us is so much more than a mere ego. The evidence for a higher yearning can be seen when thought is still and gentle. One of the oldest books in the world, the I Ching, points out that "stillness is the mountain." When we view ourselves and others from the vantage point of a quiet mind, we see how small indeed is our negativity, a mere shadow hiding out of sight of the rising sun.

Fear of the Present

The discontent, anxiety, and pointless mental chatter so common to most people's experience come in large part from preoccupation with the past and future. Another word for quiet is "now." Our fear of what we will find in the present keeps us from seeking its steadier ground and broader view. Growing up in a culture that avoids the present, we naturally conclude there must be good reason for doing so. Coupled with old suspicion are the unpleasant factors that bring most of us into the present—sudden emotional shock or physical pain. The present doesn't have a good track record in most people's lives.

Our fear of now, which is exhibited in our unwillingness to stop and look, will always hold us back from opportunities or hurry us beyond reach of them. Mentally we are in the habit of oscillating between a state of anticipation and disappointment, like waves that break against a shore, accomplish little, then turn back on themselves. When we do act, we practice a kind of victimhood or else pursue a goal that, when it arrives, is without real significance and enduring satisfaction. A rushing after, a turning away. Only the form varies. Yet the basic pattern remains undisturbed. Anything, anything at all, is preferable to mentally settling down in the present.

Even though we have stumbled over the present all our lives, we have not yet fully acknowledged it. We know the words that describe it, but we have not stooped down and taken this reality into our hands and gazed at its overwhelming brilliance. Perhaps it's because we sense that if we were to do this, we would never again be the same. Yet how harmless, how completely innocent, is the fact that the present is real.

Our life makes contact with us at the point known as "now." We cannot connect with what is over or yet to come. Now is the place where we break out of time and into reality. To the degree that our thoughts are lost in past regrets and future scheming, we are not living—in fact we are approaching death. This is not a sin, but it's definitely an unhappy way to proceed. Our actual life span is composed of an unbroken series of nows, and its quality is determined by how well we respond to present reality. Yet most of us don't even see the only instant there is.

Bluntly Put

For just a moment, allow me to be very direct. I want to ask you a few questions. Please do not be offended.

When will you stop fighting your appearance? When will you enjoy your child? Will there ever be a time in your life to drink in what your friends have to offer—it seems so little, but have you received even that little? When will you first feel a breeze passing over your cheek? Will there finally come a meal in which you will taste, really taste, your food? Just where are you going anyway? All you will ever discover about the future is that it remains the future—and so why do you still turn it over and over in your mind like some delicacy? This life of yours is not an easy habit to break, but do you really wish to continue missing almost everything of value only to end up on your deathbed wondering why you never took the time to love?

You and I no longer have time for games. Let us be done with guilt and fear. There is a song to sing. There is life to live and people to enjoy. In your heart you know that something lies beyond all this pettiness and chaos. It really is possible to live in this world and still be happy. Far more than that is possible, but let us begin with that.

We are speaking here of your *approach* to life. You are not yet approaching it because you have not yet recognized where it lies. Where is happiness found? You have a thousand assumptions about this you have not yet questioned. You are currently living those assumptions. Almost everything you think and do stems from them. And that is the way it has always been. If this book is to be different, you must understand one thing: It will take enormous effort for you to walk past your ordinary way of doing things. And yet, once you have decided to make the effort, and have committed yourself completely, all of it will eventually become surprisingly easy. Martyrdom, drudgery, testiness, suffering, tension have nothing whatsoever to do with the effort you must make. There is no organization to join, no doctrine to subscribe to, no person or book to follow, no cause to give money to. A decision must be made. It can be made now. It is simply this: "I will begin."

And what must you begin? You must try to be kind now—not appear kind, but *be* kind. You must make the effort—no, the struggle—to be happy now, and not first gain what you need in order to be happy. Some people have an experience, such as a narrow escape from death, in which they suddenly see the importance of opening their hearts to the present. And for a time they are transformed. But so often this fades and is lost, and they are left not really knowing why it passed. This must not happen to you. You cannot just add what I am talking about to your life. It must *be* your life.

Your goal to be happy, and kind, and at peace will allow for no secondary aim. You cannot hope to bring your life to peace and also take time out to be irritated. Irritation doesn't add to your chances for happiness. Of course you will make mistakes, in fact you must lose your fear of making them. But now your life purpose will be so firmly rooted in your heart that any time you recognize an error, you will unfailingly return to the only thing that matters. And what is that?

The words are so flimsy. An experience is needed to give them substance. Consistent effort will bring you that experience. Just a slight glimmer at first. A kind of happiness you had forgotten was possible. At the start of your journey it will seem to come and go as if by magic. But gradually you will begin to recognize its independence of all the happenings you thought were prerequisite. And then the moment will finally come in which it will dawn on you: "Nothing has to go right for me to be happy. People don't have to behave themselves for me to love them. I am free."

CHAPTER

4

STOPPING

The Segmented Day

The world is like a dog guarding a meatless bone. It gnaws on concepts and remains empty. The great neglected need in this era of clashing opinions is the need for direct experience. Once individuals experience a fact, they stop arguing about it because they no longer need to convince themselves of its truth. Before this simple change can take place, they must step back far enough to see the fact plainly.

For many years I have worked with people in crisis—parents in grief, batterers and battered women, rape victims, and the suicidal. Time and again I have watched even those who are desperate proceed doggedly ahead with an approach that they know in their hearts will not work. A kind of blind fear takes over, and they convince themselves that there's nothing left to try. So they stick with failure to the bitter end. They have lost their natural instinct for knowing when to stop and regain perspective.

As I began to do more counseling involving less dramatic circumstances, I noticed that the same dynamic prevailed, even with minor problems. The difficulty is almost never sustained by what the person is blaming. Solution is blocked by the failure to stop and look around.

"Here is Edward Bear, coming downstairs now, bump, bump, bump, on the back of his head, behind Christopher Robin. It is, as far as he knows, the only way of coming downstairs, but sometimes he feels that there really is another way, if only he could stop bumping for a moment and think of it." (Winnie-the-Pooh)

There are many times—far more than are recognized at first—when we get so caught up in the day's problems and events that only by pausing and intentionally stilling our thoughts will our awareness expand enough to take in all the ways we are limiting our options. To solve life's little problems, as well as most of the big ones, the first experience we need is to see what happens when the bumping stops.

Many people think they already know the benefits of pausing, but unless this practice has become as second nature as breathing, they have not yet enjoyed the benefits sufficiently.

Notice that the day comes in segments, with little beginnings and endings to each. Also notice that the mind refocuses with each change of bodily activity. This is true whether or not we finish a task. Our sense of completion varies with our sense of expectation. However thorough or incomplete we assess our efforts to be, the day still proceeds as a chain of events rather than as a continuous stream. Our mind makes a brief transition or adjustment in going from one activity to another, from sleep ending to waking up, from making the bed to getting dressed, from getting dressed to eating breakfast, and so forth. Notice, too, that there is a natural stopping point during this instant when the mind is shifting gears. It is "natural" because if done happily it facilitates and smoothes this shift as well as provides many other pleasant and more lasting benefits.

To take advantage of these transitional periods, all that's necessary is to notice them, then pause and calm the mind for a few seconds. Usually it's easier to settle the mind when the body is still. We can quietly stand where we are, or perhaps sit a moment with our eyes closed. Only an instant or two is needed.

We want a sense of the mind slowing and settling down, somewhat like coming to a stop at an intersection and allowing the car's engine to idle for a moment. We let the mind drift easily and happily. We avoid pursuing any one thought. Some individuals like to listen peacefully to the sounds around them. Others prefer to become aware of their breathing. Some like to repeat calming words such as, "My mind is quiet. I am still now." Any way of pausing is fine, provided it doesn't add a sense of burden or duty.

The Modest Work of Happiness

Have you ever, as I have, watched absentmindedly as you chose the wrong key, yet tried to insert it in the ignition or front door lock anyway? We were not thinking. Or more accurately, we were thinking rather than paying attention. It's not that we didn't know which was the correct key, but in a kind of reflexive, almost hypnotic way we picked one we often use rather than the correct one. The analogy is obvious: Everyone has the right key but very few use it consistently. In the case of happiness, the key is our undeveloped mental focus.

This is a book about the key to happiness, not the key to greater income, super health, the right friends, mental powers, model children, or all the other idols the world raises above the simple and deep enjoyment of today. As probably every child who has attended any kind of camp knows, you must "row, row, row your boat gently down the stream." And if you maintain this pace and this direction, you are guaranteed to be merry four times to every three times you row. There is definitely a way to walk through the world in peace, but attempts to change the nature of the world itself are not helpful.

If we row gently, even the rowing becomes part of our pleasure. But row we must. Stress and tedium are not required—they actually hinder—but nothing worth having will come to anyone without concentration. What makes most of our work so arid is the impossibility of the task we set before us. And this is also true of the work needed to be happy.

We insist that everything be done at once, never to be undone. We think that somehow, with a casual reading of scripture, with one good meditation, with the understanding of a few metaphysical concepts, or with the mastery of one or two spiritual practices, our life will transform and we will arrive. We actually believe there is a way it could happen in just this manner. In short, we believe in magic. So naturally our first efforts leave us feeling tired and defeated, and soon we want no more of it. And all because we expect too much of ourselves.

The world's motto is "Do little and expect much," whereas the key to genuine progress is "Work hard but expect little." It is in giving, not from giving, that we receive. Expectations merely delay because the focus of our effort is misplaced. We forget how hard and long we have worked at being unhappy and how painstakingly we have learned the rules of misery. Reversing our course can go quickly, but still the undoing must be done step by step.

The Questionable Use of Questions

A true answer is often unsophisticated, obvious, even corny. The difficulty we have, and we have plenty of it, comes from a reluctance to take what we do see and live it. We want to know in advance the details of our future course. We want an exact accounting of the results before we start. Since this is impossible, we never begin. "If you want to get there, begin" is a rule so simple that most people have immense difficulty learning it.

When I was in my early twenties, I started a real estate firm in Dallas. I took on a partner, and after a year or two of business it seemed to us we were not growing fast enough. We began seeking an investor to capitalize an expansion. Someone suggested we contact a particular Dallas businessman described as both wealthy and compassionate. That indeed was the combination of qualities we were looking for. He agreed to see us, and we gave him the details of our plan and asked if he would be interested. "You are intelligent and imaginative young men," he said. "And your plan seems sound. But I won't invest because I sense you haven't learned one basic lesson—do not spend money you don't have."

My partner and I decided he was not compassionate and quickly sought another investor. We found one and, in short, it took us five years to climb out of the financial hole we got into as a result. "Do not spend money you don't have" was too simple for us to assimilate. It is only recently—more than thirty years later—that I have become simple-minded enough to understand it.

We frequently take something as obvious as this and ask endless questions about its application and ramifications. What does "have" money mean? In the bank? What about accounts receivable? Must I always carry cash and never use a credit card? Is it wrong to lend money to others? And on and on. The unhappy part of us will not receive a simple answer. It will question it to death so that it can carry on with the same pattern that's causing the problem. Only in the calmness of our hearts can we receive what we already know and go forward.

On a higher level than spending practices, there is the familiar truth "As the sowing, the reaping" or "To give is to receive." In other words, to be at peace yourself, give peace to others. To feel loved, love. To be happy, make happy. This is very simple and is a part of all the world's inspired teachings. Yet it can be understood, accepted, and practiced only by a mind that is not agitated. Otherwise the tendency is to become mired in a thousand considerations. "Does this mean I must agree with a person who is trying to cheat me?" "Should I tell someone I am not angry when I am?" "If I give physical possessions away, will I get more?" "What about my rights, am I supposed to give those away too?" The intent of these questions is to not apply the answers. That's why this kind of questioning always produces frustration and failure.

We must become questionless. We must take a leap of faith. We must walk through the resistance we have to looking at life simply. We must not worry.

As Gayle and I discuss in detail in The Little Book of Letting Go, worry has no practical value. It is mental procrastination. It is not intuitive and doesn't protect us against making mistakes. In fact, it clouds our perspective, scatters our concentration, and makes us more prone to error.

Naturally, one does not jump from extreme to extreme. To remove fear doesn't imply foolhardiness. To remove worry doesn't imply carelessness. An absence of fear in the present leads naturally to an absence of fear later. When we are at peace, peace accompanies the effects of our choices. We apply a good answer in a good way.

The Ego/The Heart

To live happily, we need a clear sense of the difference between what I call the "heart" and the "ego." As I use the term in this book, the heart is our deepest mental level, our core of stillness and peace. It is our whole or healed mind and the seat of our innate wisdom. From this center of calmness, anything in the world can be viewed. The heart is also our store of gentleness and kindness, and we will not act harmfully, either to our selves or others, when we proceed under its influence. Through the inclusiveness or oneness of the heart, we feel not only love but also the stillness that is a part of love. With practice it is possible to have a clear sense of when our perceptions are coming from this place of quiet.

The alternative to the gentle, still urges of the heart are our conflicted, agitated ego preferences. I use the term "ego" more in an Eastern than a Freudian sense. This is generally how it's used in everyday conversation. When people speak of someone having a "big ego," the implication is that the individual feels set apart from ordinary folk.

When a person's ego grows, the nature common to all egos becomes more obvious. It's more difficult to relate to or connect with someone who has "an ego problem," and their influence on us can be disturbing. People with large egos have to some degree assumed a fake and unwholesome identity. They are not being themselves. They are not being "equal," "ordinary," "common," "real."

Like an imaginary playmate, the ego part of us can seem quite real and autonomous, but this imaginary identity does not hold our deeper feelings about anything and is therefore an untrustworthy aspect of ourselves to turn to for guidance. To the degree it motivates us, we are emotionally disconnected and unhappy.

Tricking the Mind

All the body's emotions can be triggered by fakery, as any child who has been in a carnival fun house can testify. What most people are not aware of is just how often this happens in daily life. Not every thought that passes through our mind is our true opinion. Not every emotion our body feels comes from a deep sense of self. Just as "honoring" an imaginary playmate does not give a child a true friend, so "being yourself," if this means responding from your highly unstable ego, will not put you in contact with what you genuinely feel. There is no consistent self in an ego.

There are countless examples of how the body is tricked into an inappropriate emotion: a shadow scares us, a noise makes us cringe, a cloud cover depresses us, a crying baby annoys us. If it all stopped there, perhaps no real loss of happiness would occur. Unfortunately, we often take the emotion to heart.

For example, while sitting in a waiting room we pick up a magazine and read an article on a subject we had no interest in just seconds before. Suddenly we are "made" angry over the issues raised in the article. Without fully realizing it, we carry this irritation with us for minutes or hours, and other lives are affected.

We have an experience. We feel an emotion. This much is simple. And to a large extent, it's unavoidable. However, what comes next is avoidable. We keep recalling the experience and continue feeding the emotional fire—even though that emotion is incompatible with the new situation we are now in.

In Santa Fe, Gayle and I knew a young girl who loved to watch the giant cranes, which are a rare sight in a city with so few tall buildings. But her father, who on most occasions had no difficulty joining in on her fun, could not share her enthusiasm because of a story he once heard about a crane collapsing and crushing many people. He didn't know for sure it was true, and his little girl had heard the story the same time he did. Yet for him it remained a powerful enough image to pollute the present.

Was this father a victim? We behave as though we have no alternative to this common dynamic. We believe that we have been "made" wary (angry, scared, sad, jealous) and there is little we can do about it. A surprisingly large percentage of our mental activity is spent reviewing what happened between us and someone else. Yet very little attention is given the relationship at hand. Even the individual who stands before us now is often more remembered than seen.

When we recall an encounter that in some way seems unfinished, for instance a conversation that continues as an irritant or embarrassment, we are dealing entirely with thought. We are not really a victim of the past. The past is over. Only when we recall the past in a disturbing way can it disrupt our present mental state.

Tracking the Mind

Anything that takes the edge off of a thought about the past, anything that removes the component of the thought that shatters our peace is sufficient to protect our mental wholeness. Removing the edge entails at least two steps.

First, we become aware of the line of thought that is doing the damage. Often this is not easily accomplished because it is tightly intertwined with thoughts of justification and victimization.

Second, we stop pursing the thought; we stop thinking along those lines. But this can't be done sincerely unless we distrust the premise of the thought. If we believe something yet refuse to think about it, that belief continues operating in our mind unwatched. It still affects our mood and behavior, but now we are unaware of the source. Anything we believe deeply, we will act on, no matter how irrational the belief is seen to be when consciously considered.

For example, let's say my job includes supervising someone of a different race. One day I catch myself thinking prejudicially of that person, and I am shocked that I am capable of such thoughts. If in the future I merely shy away from those thoughts and quickly think of something else whenever they nudge into consciousness, my prejudice remains intact and my dealings with this person are unconsciously tainted.

Perhaps we all know one or two individuals who don't like members of the opposite sex. Yet if you call them on it, they deny it's true. They don't want to think of themselves as small-minded, so they avoid looking at the evidence that is already in their mind, the evidence that is apparent to everyone but them.

Our goal need not be to "integrate" the split sides of our mind. It is perhaps best to leave the pollution in one place where we can keep our eye on it. But we do wish to extend our sanity into the ego part of our mind. Prejudice, impatience, anxiety, jealousy, guilt, and other forms of mental misery do not *have* to remain coiled to strike. A strong mental state is ours if we patiently undertake the process necessary to attain it.

As individuals we carry individual patterns of belief with us, yet most of us have no real knowledge of what those might be. We assume that our mind is simply as it is and we can't escape it. This is just the house we live in. Unfortunately it was designed by someone else. Even though its rooms are cramped and confused, and the walls despairingly bleak, its arrangement must go unquestioned.

Believing that our mental attributes are preset, we don't bother to explore them. But thinking within an unexplored mind is as dangerous as walking in a minefield or crossing a busy street blindfolded. We never know what emotions and impulses are likely to hit us at any given moment. By way of illustration, try predicting what mood you will be in just 5 minutes from now.

We find ourselves overreacting and don't know why. We discover that we have slipped into irritation, depression, resentment, or sadness and have no clue what mental footpath got us there. Sometimes our thoughts strengthen and comfort us, other times they enervate. We are split between happiness and unhappiness, and we have interchanged the two so frequently that we are confused as to what genuine happiness feels like and are blind to the major themes of our thoughts—even though these themes set the tone of our day.

If we are ever to be free, we must learn to track our mind as we would an unknown animal. We must come to know its habitats, its stopping points, where it always wanders into trouble, and what the places of rest and nourishment are that it invariably skirts.

Uniting the Mind

One helpful habit is to pause whenever we notice mental distress or inner conflict. Returning our mind to the present will of itself sometimes break our link with past patterns. Of course it depends on whether that is our intent. Stopping in itself is merely not continuing. Stepping back is at times essential, but we must step back into stillness or very little will change. Stillness is an attribute of the mind that can be felt and employed. When we are inwardly calm, provided the calmness is tolerant and kind, we are "in our right mind" and are automatically in position to do much good, especially for ourselves.

When working with our own mind, most of us have a tendency to judge it and jump to conclusions about how it needs to change. When we feel judgmental in this way, we are criticizing our mind with our mind. All we accomplish is to enlarge the split. The mind is helped by extending sanity, never by attacking insanity. It's important not to allow a sense of battling yourself to develop, despite how often this course of action is celebrated in plays, comic books, novels, and movies.

We are not attempting to change the mind but merely to watch it carefully in order to increase our knowledge of its system of beliefs. Since our goal is increased awareness, it is essential not to decide beforehand what beliefs should, or should not, be there. If you already have opinions on this, see if you can suspend them during the periods when you watch your mind. Before you begin, perhaps say to yourself, "I am not deciding what is a good or bad belief. I am looking at my thoughts as if seeing them for the first time."

During your periods of quiet watching, the attitude you want is similar to one you may have had as a child when you would lie on your back and watch the shapes clouds took. There was neither approval nor disapproval involved, just relaxed interest. Another image that some find helpful is to watch your beliefs much like you might stand aside and study the characters in a passing parade.

It should be noted that the mind tends to become quiet when watched. It may take a few moments for thoughts definite enough to recognize to begin coming. Should you start to feel anxious about the duration of stillness, you can try recalling some recent thoughts, or you might pick a few subjects at random to think about. But return to allowing your mind to be spontaneous as soon as possible.

To heal our mental split we need increased awareness of the split itself. Our mind does no less than determine whether life is worth living. Yet we can't change even one detail of our mental conflict unless we know what that detail is. Strictly speaking, we have only one mind, but that it is divided should be painfully clear. It can be quite helpful to view our lower mind from our higher mind, to look carefully at our ego from the standpoint of our heart.

The practice of watching our beliefs, because it is unintrusive, includes a powerful corrective force. To watch is to extend. The watcher (our heart or peaceful mind) enters what is watched (our ego or agitated mind) and transforms it the way light streaming through opening curtains transforms a room that had been deep in shadow. This experience can't be forced, but with a little practice an expanding sense of peace should begin accompanying these quiet pauses in which the present contents of your mind are calmly observed.

Although it is a discovery process that can take many months or years, once we are aware of our specific ego beliefs, we begin to see what happens when we act on them. We acknowledge the damage we cause ourselves and others. Going back to the example of the prejudiced supervisor, once this person takes responsibility for his or her beliefs about certain groups of people, the painful consequences are immediately apparent each time those beliefs influence the supervisor's actions. In this way the beliefs composing the prejudice are brought into question.

We can't destroy our basic beliefs, no matter how insane they are. The ego part of us can't be perfected, only relinquished. We gradually learn to distrust it and decline its guidance. This is a process of gradual enlightenment or increasing awareness, not internal war. If we look at alcoholism as another example, we see the same process. Just as the prejudiced supervisor first has to see and accept that he or she is prejudiced, alcoholics must first see that they are alcoholics. Acknowledging and "owning" that fact, they now come face to face with the devastation they have caused. Thus they begin to distrust their ego urge to drink. They begin to doubt their belief in the benefits of getting drunk, and sooner or later nothing is tempting about alcohol. Yet they remain "recovering" alcoholics because they understand that the basic belief in alcohol is still a part of their ego.

CHAPTER

5

BEGINNING

Reacting Blindly

Have you ever hypnotized a chicken? When I was a boy I lived part of each year on a farm. At that time chickens had not been domesticated to the degree they are now, and these somewhat wild birds fascinated me. When fried chicken was planned for dinner, the hen that had been chosen to fulfill this brightest dream of all loyal chickens would in the course of the day find herself without a head. But this was not an immediate tragedy, because such is the nature of the chicken that it can run around quite well without a head, at least for a time.

The roosters were also slightly beyond belief. They apparently had only three goals in life: to eat, to fertilize eggs, and to attack anything that moved. Of course, these are not uncommon goals. What was uncommon was the rooster's single-minded determination to pursue them. I have known a cock to be knocked cold with a grain bucket, come to, and instantly attack again, and to continue this until the villainous egg gatherer had left the coop.

Thankfully I was never assigned the tasks of fighting roosters or wringing hens' necks, but I was allowed to hypnotize as many chickens as I wished. The hardest part was to catch them, for in those days they could fly quite well. After that the rest was simple. You merely hold the chicken's chin flat against the ground and with your finger or a stick draw a line straight out from its beak. It will watch the line form in the dirt, and even though you release it, so fixed is the chicken's attention on the line that it will stay frozen in position as though still being firmly held. Once its attention turns to itself (at your urging or in due time), it realizes it is free and runs off.

We are like chickens in that as long as we are preoccupied with what is outside of us, we are locked in our own self-styled prison. Yet when our awareness returns to what we have within, we realize that we are free.

If we continue reacting to the world the way we always have, we remain its victim. The key isn't to fight against our reactions. That approach is interminable. Instead, we must see that our reactions are a choice, and we must choose to be heart-motivated. Only then will we cease being some particle of paper tossed by every worldly breeze.

Reactions use the contradictory past as guide instead of the gentle, unified preferences that come from the heart's peace. We are never free of our erraticism as long as some aspect of the world manipulates us at will.

Declining to react blindly doesn't mean we neglect needed repairs, refuse to shop in advance for meals, or resist being shocked or saddened by another's tragedy. Anticipating our peace of mind and doing in the present what needs to be done to protect it is not the same as coming under the spell of events. Our tendency to react blindly isn't nourished by viewing the day calmly. Looking at things honestly and quietly leads to well-considered overt acts as easily as it does to patient waiting.

Unquestionably, one of the keys to happiness is to let our first reaction be stillness.

Our life reflects the unity or division of our will. Either we decide life or it decides us. In one, choice is strength and hope based on vision. In the other, there is only spreading impotence and frustration. All too often isolation and physical misery dominate the closing years and months of a lifetime. They descend slowly, like a vast and final curtain on a play that never reached a denouement or even had a single meaning for anyone. Because a decision was not made, life just happened. Loneliness and bewilderment were inevitable because a real alternative was never sought.

The Power of Decision

If a decision about life is possible, and indeed it is, there must be something outside of life, or at least outside of life as we ordinarily view it. If the way you think about your day determines the kind of day you have, you must be more than your day. The mind that decides to decide gradually moves into that realm that is more than a day, more even than a single life, and far more than our daily peck of troubles.

The ability to decide is merely the ability to give attention. Whether we realize it or not at the time, we have *chosen* to look at whatever "has our attention" and have decided to turn away from everything else. Such mental focus is perhaps the most powerful force on Earth. This was overwhelmingly demonstrated at the turn of the millennium and after the terrorist attacks of September 11, 2001.

As 1999 became 2000, the world's population turned its attention toward one simple idea: "We will celebrate the new millennium!" And the results were beyond anyone's imagining. Despite millions of people being pressed into crowds for hours, despite fears of a worldwide computer disaster, despite profound cultural and religious differences, despite even the dictates of different calendars, we experienced the impossible—peace on Earth for 24 hours.

And in America, a country that over several decades had fragmented into profound selfishness and separation, when the unthinkable tragedy occurred, when national symbols and thousands of innocent people were almost instantly destroyed, the nation turned its attention toward one simple idea: "We want to help." Within days, before political and religious leaders had yet called for generosity, tens of millions of dollars had poured into charities and thousands of volunteers had poured into New York City. Our nation felt what it had long forgotten, that our country is a family, that we are united, and what is done to some of us is done to us all.

What we give our full attention to is what we decide. We are what we perceive and how we perceive it. This merely states the obvious, but we must not underestimate our ability to overlook the obvious.

Indecision, a Form of Choosing

Even though the mind exists, it can imagine itself as anything, and quite obviously does, for example in dreams and fantasies. The cause of these illusions, and one factor that gives them their appeal, is unquestioned judgment—criticism, comparison, righteousness. When we feel competitive with another person, we believe that we are separate from that individual. Thus division is introduced into a mind that is naturally whole and it begins to fragment and project. But when the mind stops appraising and ranking, it reassumes its natural function of wholeness or love.

Love has no singular, small, unconnected target. Nothing is

outside of love because it *wishes* nothing outside of it. Yet these words are virtually meaningless without an accompanying experience. And every experience is preceded by a decision.

Letting our day dictate our mood is a decision. "Indecision" is a deliberate choice that the status quo continue, that there be still more versions of what has always been, that nothing new start now. Confusion about what to be in life is disbelief in love. So we must keep in mind that to decide our day is not to declare war on events or other people's behavior.

Deciding to have the kind of day we want doesn't give us special powers and advantages over those who don't yet know enough to decide. It never calls for us to wring from other people their compliance by nagging or out-reasoning them. If we try to decide against certain circumstances occurring today, we will lose. But if we peacefully and kindly plan how to bypass their usual impact on our emotions, we will win.

Even to want personal advantage is a joyless state because of the sense of estrangement it entails. By consciously choosing to be happy, we leave the battlefield altogether. Why would we incessantly skirmish over how things should go and people should be if we knew that a great field of peace surrounds these tiny places of war? All we have to do to enter this field is decide that we would rather be happy than right. In order for this to occur, the hypnotic hold of war must first give way to a greater interest in peace.

Conflict over Food and Everything Else

It takes much practice to be able to ask ourselves a simple question and without guilt, without anxiety, come to a decision about which we feel peaceful. Most of us decide in conflict, act in conflict, and think this is the way life must be. Mixed feelings arise from a sense of having more than one self. On the surface this appears to be the inevitable outcome of our personal history. Since we have had many opposing experiences, it seems natural that we are divided about almost everything.

Take food, for example. Very few children escape, on the one hand, a series of running battles with their parents over what, when, and how much they should eat and, on the other hand, being presented special foods as a reward or as part of a celebration. Usually these "wonderful" foods are the very ones over which issues had been made on previous occasions. The resulting lesson that children learn about a surprising number of things is "I want it, but I shouldn't want it."

In the case of food some parents realize that there are alternatives to these daily wars that ruin mealtimes for everyone and can color an entire childhood. Most children can do quite well on remarkably poor diets, and even though the parent should unquestionably make the diet as wholesome as possible, it must be remembered that anxiety and chronic unhappiness also affect health. Often children are not as hungry by evening as adults are, and it's frequently unrealistic to expect them to eat their major meal then. We all know how hard it is to abandon our eating preferences, so why wage these battles with our children over precise manners and over tasting every last thing? Yet most of us doggedly continue teaching our children conflict in this area and a hundred others.

If our approach as parents is not enough to cause conflicted feelings about food, thrown into the child's life are inconsistent messages from TV, schoolteachers, and friends about what foods are nutritious ("make you grow up tall and strong") or, in the case of TV ads, give you all variety of magical attributes. As the child becomes an adult, inevitably there are bad experiences with food along the way. Food poisoning at a restaurant. Taste reactions from overindulgence. Unexpected weight gain from a change in diet. Allergies.

Indigestion. Plus the constant glut of contradictory articles and pronouncements on exactly what should always be and should never be eaten, until finally a single attitude toward anything edible becomes impossible.

Up to this moment I have either heard or read stern warnings from one or more experts against the following foods, all of which I had previously been taught were "natural" and completely safe: tomatoes, potatoes, eggplant (and other nightshade plants), avocados, mushrooms, any raw vegetable, certain cooked vegetables, bell peppers, all nuts, milk (in fact, all dairy products), beans (except green), beef, shellfish, commercially raised chickens, eggs, vegetable oils, whole or refined wheat, dried, cooked, or raw bananas, any fresh fruit or fruit juices, and carrots "in excess." I can't recall having read anything against rutabaga or okra, but then these are not hot topics. I'm sure that by just being mentioned in a book the necessary research will now commence and these two vegetables, cooked or raw, will be stripped of their cloak of innocence.

Again, our daily decisions concerning food are just one area of chronic conflict. Almost everything else about which we make decisions—picking out the "right" presents to give, shopping for a car, choosing a spouse, deciding how much time to exercise, knowing when to step in and direct our children and when to step back and let them learn for themselves—could easily be shown to hold vast unconscious conflict for the average person. Possibly the only thing we can still do without conflict is have a diarrhea attack. When that happens we seem to know exactly what to do and there are no second thoughts.

By merely having had previous experiences around anything, we are rendered divided as to how to approach whatever choice we think is called for. Our habit is to quickly find some grounds for a decision, to act, then as the lessons from our contradictory past push toward the surface of our mind, to worry at length about what we have just done. And all of this seems not only normal but also unavoidable.

What Has to Be Done Today?

We sit at the table of life with an unacknowledged guest. We think that by not looking at or speaking to him we protect ourselves from his influence. Because we refuse to see, we don't acknowledge that this guest sprinkles poison on every bite we eat, every sip we drink. If we were to gaze honestly at him, we would indeed be horrified, for we would see ourself.

Power is not in positive thinking but in negative thinking. Power is a phoenix that again and again rises from ashes. But not just any ashes. Feathered in gold and royal purple, singular and separate in its magnificence, the phoenix will cease to exist unless it self-immolates. Only in looking at our most petty, malevolent, and embarrassing thoughts—and seeing the harm they have caused—are we reborn with a pure heart. This process is usually long, essentially unpleasant, and at the time feels self-destructive. Yet the effect of remaining unaware of our darker thought patterns must be seen before we can hope for sustained happiness. Until we ignite this fire of purification, oneness with others, enjoyment of life, and an inner state of well-being will magically come and go.

Set an alarm for a random time, and when it goes off later in the day, stop and ask yourself what you have been thinking about, what has been the drift of your thoughts—for just the past 10 minutes. Anyone who does this two or three times for just one day will recognize how deep is our habit of allowing our mind to operate in the dark. Then the only question will be, Does it really matter what we think?

Possibly you believe it's important to know how you spend your time and to stay "on task." Maybe you consider yourself efficient. Unfortunately, I can't say that about myself, but I know people who consistently organize and execute well. Perhaps it matters to you where your money goes. Your bank balance seldom surprises you. Again, I have not done well in this area either, but I know those who have. Maybe you keep track of what you put into your body. I do a little better at this, but still I have had the thought many times in my life, "There must be something wrong with these scales."

Another familiar thought of mine is, "I haven't even started. Where did the day go?" Then there is the more ominous thought, "I haven't even started. Where did my life go?" That's the one I hope I won't have to say on my deathbed. Because the answer will be, "You don't know because you never loved your life enough to notice what controls its direction. You never noticed the part that your mind played in every step you ever took. And since you didn't notice, your life wandered aimlessly and went nowhere."

Purpose

A Single Reason for Living

Before the subjective mess that most of our lives are in can be cleaned up, a single life purpose must take the place of variable conflicting goals. It is the activity of multiple goals that stirs up the mind.

An unhurried mind is content and is a definite improvement. But only a still mind is deeply happy. To reach this state we must come to have one, whole, all-encompassing reason for being alive. This reason has to come from an experience of the heart and not from just mastering a concept.

A major breakthrough has occurred when the answerless question "What is the best way?" has been put aside out of love for the destination. Perhaps you are like me in that you have already changed your "way" enough to recognize that "to search for the truth" is one of our favorite delaying tactics. The truth is true, and it is so obvious that it's understood by little children. Let us stop looking for still one more way to say it. Let us begin to practice what we already know.

The single purpose that everyone shares on a heart level can be stated, and has been given down the years, in myriad forms. The phrasing is not important, but it is helpful if we can think of it in a way that is simple and clear and in a form that pleases us, even though from time to time we may want to change the words.

It is never required that our purpose be expressed in spiritual or religious terms. Because of the unhappy experiences many have had with this kind of language, it would be a hindrance for those individuals to use it. Many others love the traditional language of devotion, and it helps them focus. In short, the exact way we express our life purpose is not perfectible. There are no right or wrong words, since what is true applies to everything.

Over many years I visited my mother in a series of alcoholic treatment centers, until, in her mid-fifties, she stopped drinking. Reputedly the most successful center in the country was run by a former alcoholic who turned lives around primarily through daily speeches that he gave to the assembled clients. He was a dynamic speaker who used every oratory trick I had ever heard of. But the first time I listened to him speak, I kept waiting in vain for the Big Concept that was performing the miracle cures I had been hearing about. The central theme of this talk and every one I heard thereafter was always the same: "Make your only goal in life to be a decent human being." Now I look back and realize that one simple thought such as this is the only spiritual path that any of us needs—if we are willing to practice it daily.

Perhaps the oldest and most universally practiced path is the thought that we should treat others as we would be treated. Surely nothing more would be needed if we took this to heart. Today another commonly used statement of a life goal has come to be known as "the prayer of Saint Francis." I have seen it written in several forms. This one is perhaps the simplest.

> Today, let me be an instrument of Thy peace.
> Where there is hatred, let me sow love,
> Where there is injury, pardon;
> Where there is discord, union;
> Where there is doubt, faith;
> Where there is darkness, light;
> Where there is sadness, joy.
> May I not so much seek
> To be consoled, as to console;
> To be understood, as to understand;
> To be loved, as to love.
> For it is in giving that we receive.
> It is in pardoning that we are pardoned.
> And it is in dying to self
> That we are born to eternal life.

For some this prayer is impossibly demanding. It seems to be asking them to become a saint who walks the Earth in absolute purity. But if you know a few of the details of Saint Francis's life, you understand that the prayer states the yearnings of his heart and is assuredly not a description of what he was able to achieve each day. Our ultimate goal, even our daily goal, can indeed be perfect—if we are patient enough with ourselves to ensure a steady and consistent advance.

We are expecting too much of ourselves if we think we can go even a few hours without making mistakes. Still, our many mistakes must not become grounds for discouragement. Discouragement, even when it comes in the wake of striving for perfection, is the love of unhappiness, because that is what it turns back to as its alternative. All we can do is the best we can in the present. Yet we are always capable of doing better.

Our Pre-existing Mindset

Today, as every day, we stand at a crossroad. One direction makes us part of the solution to the world's immense and protracted suffering. The other perpetuates our ancient and exhausting task of adding to it.

How few there are who make life easier on other people! For the most part we needlessly complicate the lives of those around us. The sum of our effect is an added degree of hassle or worry, or worse. If we are honest, we know that we confuse and tire even our own children. In the ways we relate to family and friends, we are usually a burden and at best, unreliably so.

This book asks that you join with those who want to be a consistent comfort to their loved ones. Speaking for myself, I cannot look at my life and say that I was a blessing to those who knew me. In fact, I can think of no one who was consistently blessed by being a close friend or relative of mine. I have done better with acquaintances, but does that really matter? I have needlessly hurt scores of former friends and family members. I can also say that I am determined to use the days I have left to try to erase my dark footsteps with a little light. I now realize that this can only be done today. And it begins with the thoughts I choose upon awakening each morning—not the concepts with which I fill my mind, but the deep beliefs already within me that I select from.

I know from many reinforcing experiences that none of us reverses our daily patterns without taking enough time to feel our sincerity. We kid ourselves if we think we can wake up and fill our minds with worries about what we did yesterday and concerns about what has to be done today and still not be a source of concern and worry to those we will encounter. How can we possibly bring comfort to others when our mind is scattered among multiple self-oriented goals?

Most of us have a different goal within each situation and activity. Maybe this in itself would not be so limiting if it weren't for the fact that we don't set the goal beforehand. The event sets it for us. It's interesting to notice that we are in the habit of thinking certain lines of thought as we look in the mirror, other lines while washing our body, and still others while dressing, eating breakfast, and so on. Clearly we have a physical routine, but just as rigid is our mental routine.

For example, just after waking up we may keep our body still a moment while our mind quickly surveys it. We are taking account of how we feel, and this roving of our attention over the various parts of the body is so rapid and automatic that many people who do this regularly may never have noticed it, even though that one act begins setting their priorities for the day. If nothing else, they begin with the basic conviction that they are a separate, unconnected body rather than a deeply connected mind or spirit.

When I first began watching my initial thoughts, I discovered that every morning I was toting up the hours of sleep I had gotten. This habit probably started when our son John used to wake us up during the night to discuss on-the-spot dreams and couldn't possibly imagine our not wanting to hear every detail. When I stopped looking at the clock before climbing into bed, and in the morning stopped trying to guess at how much rest I had gotten, I began noticing a small increase in freedom from the oppression of time. This in turn led to an increased awareness of how pervasive time considerations were for me personally.

My God was not God, it was the clock. This is not an original insight, but it was an important one for me. Contrary to the fear I have heard expressed about this type of observation, it did not lead to carelessness about being on time or a diminished respect for other people's time values. It simply gave me an option I had not allowed myself before. I found myself asking, "If time is not the most important consideration within this situation, what is?"

Perhaps neither a body-oriented nor a time-oriented purpose will be one of many you discover that you are unconsciously setting every morning, but unless you have already increased your awareness of your first mental activities, you have some nice gains in freedom in store for you.

Our mental regimen in the morning sets our operational mode. It centers us within a mindset that will not be altered without far more effort than it would have taken to start the day differently. The first step is to identify the old thought patterns connected to waking up, walking to the bathroom, taking a shower, walking to the kitchen, opening the refrigerator door, and the like. And the second step is to interrupt these patterns. Fortunately, all that is needed to interrupt them is full awareness of what they are.

Given enough awareness, the mind is self-correcting. A battle of one set of thoughts against another set is not only unnecessary but also counterproductive. We don't need to pour positive ideas on top of our existing mental content. That practice actually diminishes awareness. All we need do is look at what we are already thinking. Unless we take time to identify the mental tone we usually set, and how we set it, we see no real reason to correct it.

One Daily Priority

Having noticed our profound habit of operating from a series of unconsciously set, conflicting goals, we naturally want a better approach. One simple way to attain this is to decide what kind of person we want to be before the day decides for us.

Luckily everyone wakes from sleep with at least an instant or two of mental stillness. One of the first thoughts that breaks this stillness can be preplanned. We can decide before lying down to sleep what our waking purpose will be. This can be any idea we choose. And because we choose it, and because it comes into our quiet awakening mind, there is no battle with other thoughts or purposes, as there can be when we try to superimpose a daily purpose after having already launched into the day's activities.

Try this simple experiment. Just before lying down, formulate your purpose for the next day. You can put an idea into your own words, choose from the ones listed below, or pick one from numerous books and calendars of daily thoughts. How you arrive at it is not critical, but be certain it is a purpose that will cover everything, one that can use anything that happens to its own end.

If for instance you were to choose "Today I will judge nothing that occurs" from *A Course in Miracles,* you can see that no matter how outrageous the occurrence, it will still serve your aim of not judging. In fact, the more outrageous it is, the more interesting might be the challenge of applying your single goal. Whether this would be true for you or not, to take on the job of judging nothing will give you all the mental work you could possibly want for one day. And should you succeed even for a few scattered moments, it will be one of the happiest days you have yet experienced. It may not be obvious why that should be, but anyone who makes a sincere effort at setting and carrying out a single daily aim, for just a few days, will experience a profound difference in their mental tone.

Here are a few examples of the kinds of unifying thoughts you might use. Only one idea should be practiced per day, and often there is a deepening effect in continuing it for several days.

"I will do all things in peace."

"I would rather be happy than right."

"I will follow my peaceful preference."

"I can know peace wherever I am."

"My interpretations are my world."

"Nothing has to go right today for me to be happy."

"Peace is my decision."

"What do I want this to mean?"

"The key to happiness is a quiet mind."

"To comfort is all I seek."

"Today I will be kind."

"I will remain in the present."

When you start to wake, slowly begin repeating your purpose. Let your mind move past the words to your intent. Then sit up and begin building your resolve to follow your purpose throughout the day. Although this need take only a few moments, do not start your usual activities until you know that your purpose is firmly set and that you are sure it is what you wish to strive for above all else.

It is best not to tell yourself what conduct your purpose demands of you. You are setting a mental tone and not fantasizing outward reactions. It will be more in line with your aim to allow your actions to flow naturally from your attitude. In this respect, your morning decision is to leave yourself alone.

Do not, for example, use your quiet period in the morning to rehearse what you should say to others. Instead, picture the kinds of things that are likely to happen today and see yourself responding from a new place within you, a temperament that is as gentle and free as it is certain of its way.

Picturing the tone you wish to carry throughout the day is a fast and effective method of orienting the mind toward happiness and building a reserve of strength that you can quickly fall back on whenever your happiness begins slipping away. Each time you forget to follow your purpose, merely remember. Don't waste one second regretting having forgotten. Forgetting calls only for remembering. By gently starting over in this way, you will gradually come to know your still and united mind, and what every prophet, saint, and sage has said since time began will dawn on you as true. You will know that you are a part of something greater than yourself. And this will make you happy.

CHAPTER

7

THE DAY

Routing Around Mistakes

In the early stages of reorienting our mind, it's common to forget repeatedly the purpose we set that morning. This does not hurt our progress provided we begin again as soon as we realize what has happened. But like an angry child, our usual response is to knock over the whole tower of blocks because one or two fell. Thus the tendency we must watch is to count the day lost because we have already made several obvious mistakes. We may even have been aware of a mistake at the time we were making it, tried halfheartedly to check ourselves, then "willfully" continued being wrong. None of that matters provided we start the day over as soon as we notice that we are once again strong enough to do so.

It is not making a mistake but dwelling on it that delays us. The key is to look at how far we have come rather than how far we have to go. Our motivation is up to us. In my opinion, the Divine does not "kick us in the pants" to get us back on track, and we should not wait around for a higher power to take responsibility.

The unhappy part of our mind thinks that self-criticism is virtuous, a form of humility and a worthy indication of "being honest with yourself." It is forever engaged in trying to understand and trying to explain. Yet to attempt to understand a mistake is simply to make another mistake. You will have eliminated one of the most pervasive hindrances to growth when you learn to react to every error, no matter what its degree or persistence, by simply acknowledging it and beginning again.

A major help in this direction is routine. A settled daily pattern allows our momentum to build more quickly because a good plan can route us around foreseeable entanglements. Having no clear idea of what we wish to do, we are inclined to be hesitant about almost everything, and the situations that have previously called to our unhappiness continue to do so because they still are not receiving our full attention. The day happens to us, and its only meaning is in whether we like or dislike what has just occurred. Thus we put ourself in a position where all we can do is await the outcome. Since very few moments are perceived as pure outcome, we spend most of our life waiting.

Within a day approached in this indecisive way there will be a greater number of unexpected and unusual occurrences. Many people think they like to view these as adventures, but we must realize that even if we are excited, we continue more or less as a victim of the general course of things, circumstances remain heavily weighted, and our happiness is contingent. Being caught off guard doesn't actually increase freedom. Freedom is rarely found in abandon or momentary impulse.

Everyone's day has some routine, but often it's merely a pattern that has grown up unexamined and is an aid to nothing in particular. It is not happy to incessantly make and remake rules about how life should be, as so often parents do with children and inwardly do with themselves. If the basic plan of our day has been simply and intelligently set out, we are relieved of many shallow decisions and it is less difficult for our thoughts to turn to peace.

The body demands less of our attention if we allow for such obvious factors as how regularly we need to eat, what foods we should avoid because they make us anxious, and how much sleep and exercise we require in order to feel good. If a type of TV program, having lunch with a particular person, phone calls at certain hours, house guests, or too many social engagements stir us up to the point where concentrating on our purpose for the day becomes difficult, our life *can* be adjusted so that many of these unproductive involvements are sidestepped.

It's obviously not the function of this book to lay out a model daily routine, even if such were possible. To even mention the desirability of coming up with a plan that avoids obvious pitfalls runs the risk of strengthening our ancient penchant for external solutions and our appetite for rules and strictures. There are no external solutions, except temporary ones to external problems, and of course unhappiness is not an external problem.

If the real purpose of a daily routine is kept in mind, it won't become a little god that everyone around us must kneel before. A rigid routine makes no sense. Our firmness should lie in our resolve to be and make happy. We can have consistent behavior or we can have a consistent mental state, but we can't have both. Our daily plan is here to make life easier on us and our loved ones and must therefore accommodate shifts in circumstance. If, for instance, on some morning our scheduled quiet time would be an inconvenience to a member of our family, we don't achieve our goal by insisting that this person wait in distress while we practice serenity on time.

Sidestepping Stimuli

The Eastern mystical tradition of withdrawing from ego-provoking stimuli, although misinterpreted in the West as turning one's back on the world, is nevertheless an excellent antidote for one of our most common and devastating mental pollutants. Relationships founder, families split apart, and health deteriorates in the churning aftermath of overstimulation. Yet the effects of excessive activity on our internal state still goes unrecognized by most people. This has been especially true ever since our culture got being busy mixed up with being important.

"Do you think you should call him—he's a very busy person?" Translation: "He's more important than you." During a bullet-riddled rescue scene in an action film made several years ago, a man shouts to his fellow combatant, "You're bleeding!" To which the other shouts back, "I don't have time to bleed." That's just how busy most people think they would like to be. "I'd rather be busy than happy" now stands along side of "I'd rather be right than happy" as perhaps the two main supporting columns of present-day human misery.

Being preoccupied with surrounding conditions, we are consequently influenced by them. It's irrelevant that people and circumstances should not be able to distract us if in fact they do. Even though we are vulnerable to much of the world, we can minimize its effects on us, and we can do so far beyond what we conceive is feasible when we first set out. The possibilities for cutting back and simplifying are enormous and actually appear to expand as we proceed.

Without ever meeting you, I can tell you one hard fact about your lifestyle. *You are doing too much.* Even if you consider yourself an indolent person, you are being overstimulated and need to step back. This statement sounds absurd because of our habit of characterizing activities such as sleeping, watching TV, eating, sitting, taking long baths, chatting on the phone, and so on as "not doing anything," meaning "not producing anything." The typical unconscious judgment is actually more specific than this. In our culture any activity that does not lead to money is looked down on. It's difficult for most people to clean their house or care for their children for a sustained period without becoming annoyed or depressed. The prevailing attitude is that unless there is the possibility of monetary gain in the end, our time is being poorly spent.

Regardless of the popular notions of what activities constitute "not doing anything," any bodily activity produces a lingering mental disruption, however mild. All stimuli can't be eliminated, since the body is always doing something, but some activities are clearly less inwardly disruptive than others. For example, starting our day with a period of quiet will create less emotional agitation than will rushing madly about. (Even being quiet will create some, as we schedule the time, find a place, assume a posture, and so on.) This is the truth that sets us free. Whenever possible, we should carefully select these stimuli.

Short of ascending out of the world altogether, there is really no final and perfect attainment in this area. Yet substantial gains await anyone who is willing to recognize that a simple, clutter-free day makes it far easier to be centered, kind, and present than does a day chuck-full of "meaningful" activities. How meaningful can an activity be if it's not done with happiness?

Acts of Grace

Perhaps it has become apparent to you that unless we carry our core of peace into a task, the task is of no lasting benefit to our loved ones or to us. Rather than adding more and more hollow deeds to a life already profoundly scattered, it seems to me that our actual responsibility is to cut back to the point where we can do a few things with grace.

Our happiness is like the first tiny green shoot of a new plant. It is fragile and vulnerable to incursions. Unless we give it space to grow, it will wither away. This has already happened too many times in all of our lives. Yet when we fail to interfere with our happiness, it begins increasing in power.

The mother and three children of a family we know were visiting relatives in Washington. One afternoon, right after the grandmother had taken a roast out of the oven, the youngest child accidentally pulled down a pan of hot grease drippings over her face and chest. The father flew from New Mexico and joined the family at the hospital. After weeks of operations and convalescence, they all found themselves driving back home, in severe debt from the costs, and still unsure how much permanent scarring their daughter would sustain. Yet they told us that during that long day in the car they were happier and more peaceful than they had been in years.

Before the visit the family's life had been hectic, and of course it had remained so during the long emergency. But driving home there was suddenly nothing to do, and the natural, almost inevitable result was an immediate surfacing of love and peace despite the considerable pall that still hung over their lives. When home was reached and life resumed as normal, just as naturally as it came their happiness began to vanish.

The only difference in this common dynamic is that this couple saw what was happening to their family and took a step to reverse it. The mom and dad made a list of each contact they and their children had with the world. Then they eliminated or cut back on every one that seemed feasible.

For many people a typical list of contacts with the world might include the following:

1. An hour of background television while getting ready for work

2. A quarter of an hour reading e-mails; one or two phone calls

3. The drive to work

4. Visual encounters with other drivers

5. One or two radio news breaks, 2 or 3 ad breaks, and talk from a radio host

6. The job itself

7. Eating at a restaurant or company lunchroom at noon

8. The drive home

9. More radio

10. More encounters with drivers

11. Stopping to pick something up on the way home

12. Stopping for gas several times a week

13. Once home, an hour making or receiving phone calls

14. An hour with e-mails

15. Watching an average of 3 or 4 hours of evening television

16. Several unexpected errands during the week

17. Inviting friends over once or twice a week

18. Going out with friends once or twice a week

19. One or two parties a month

20. Three or four meetings or appointments a month

21. An average of one movie every other weekend

22. Ten or more phone calls, 10 or more hours of television, and 1 or 2 hours on the computer every weekend

23. If they have kids, several school-related activities a week

24. Car pooling duties every week

25. Other activities with kids such as team practices, shopping for school supplies and clothes, and entertainment

Note that these activities include mostly those times when the choice is to come into contact either directly or indirectly with other people besides one's family. And of course many of these encounters are good and necessary and should not be eliminated. It is the overall volume of busyness that we wish to turn down so that our mind will have time to hear its own joy.

At first glance it may seem that nothing you are doing can be eliminated. But if you are honest with yourself you will see that this is not entirely true. Let me list a few of many cutbacks Gayle and I have made over the years. I realize that some of these most people would not want to make. The point is that almost any simplification is possible.

We reduced the number of incoming phone calls from approximately twenty a day to about ten a week. We organized our shopping and errands so that our trips in the car were probably about one-twentieth of what they had been two years before. We extricated ourselves from those "we owe them" kinds of parties and dinners. We seldom have houseguests (there was a period when we seldom did not). We now go new-car shopping (a longstanding insanity of ours) only when the old one is literally falling apart. By changing our diet and exercise habits we have reduced the number of visits to doctors.

As a consequence of these and many other simplifications, we have amassed a small fortune in time that we lavish on our children, meditations, long walks, and other what might be called "heart-oriented" activities. My income is now about half what it was before I started declining most speaking invitations, but my new riches in loving and being loved far exceed the enjoyment level of my life a few years ago. Cutting back is certainly not all there is to nurturing happiness. Yet like clearing weeds and preparing soil, it's a critical first step, a step that is often neglected in the name of one's "duty"—as if being harried and irritable could add to our peace or the peace of the world.

"Better to Face It Now"

Once we cut back on what we can, what do we do with all that's left? The current desire for body-mind-spirit advancement and metaphysical attainments has at least one unfortunate side effect. Many are thwarting their progress by believing they are beyond the average person's level of growth. This is like one figure in a dream looking at another figure and saying, "I'm more awake than you are."

When we make this mistake we begin forcing an appearance, an empty image of what we think enlightenment should look like. This puts us in conflict with our normality or equality. We think we shouldn't be afraid of a dark house. We should remain unaffected by crowded or angry places. Our latest system of diet should not make our tummies gurgle or our children's faces break out. The fur of a tiny kitten should not cause us to sneeze. And when we go camping, Nature should not make us itch.

In other words, as soon as we think we are superior to our surroundings, we are at war with them. To deny our fears and fail to recognize that activating them has mental consequences sets us up for a string of little defeats throughout the day. Perhaps common sense is not very exciting, but it does take us further than pride.

Perhaps the best way to rid our day of the turmoils that regularly plague us is to find some gentle way to walk around them. No one actually has to "learn to deal with" anything!

Certainly it may be simpler to do so under certain circumstances, but there is no specific characteristic of the world that must be mastered.

Just think for a moment how absurd is this concept of needing to "learn to cope" with everything that goes on in the world. Yet most people believe they must overcome the circumstances that arise in their daily life because "it will be good for me in the long run." Perhaps if there were only a few worldly conditions, this ideal would make sense, but the potential problems we can and will face are legion. They never come to an end. And they rarely have anything to do with what we have learned to cope with.

You would think that it would be obvious that it's *happier* to walk gently than with bloodied feet. "The easy way out"—that phrase so profane to so many—can be attended by kindness as well as by tranquility. Nothing worth having is gained through self-imposed chaos, for it's not possible to attack ourself without attacking others. Our goal is not even to improve our outward personality. That is part of the violent approach that has kept everything the same. We are simply attempting to allow more of our basic nature to surface. To do that, it is helpful to have a way of living that does not needlessly distract us from that purpose. As we have discussed, that means we must avoid useless battles. But it also means we must identify and take responsibility for our old patterns of unhappiness. Then we must move past these patterns in the simplest way possible.

Do not hesitate to turn and look straight at what usually happens to upset you. This is quite different from trying to explain our mistakes, which is impossible. Whatever the irritant or torment is, there is a way past it. Actually there are a hundred ways, and we see at least some of them when we set aside our cherished resistance, take time to look at what's going on, and are not too picky about which means we use to put the problem behind us.

Identifying Specific Patterns

Gayle and I have a friend who as a scientist has made several important discoveries. His guiding principle when taking up a new problem within his two fields of study is "Data, data, and more data." Likewise, a good place to start in dealing with any personal problem, especially a familiar pattern, is to broaden our awareness of all aspects of the difficulty. We practice looking at our life as if seeing it for the first time.

In a sense, many people start their day in perfection. They set their purpose, and their purpose is good. But soon something happens that "makes" them forget the goal. At least it appears to force them to forget or to discard their purpose. That in itself should tell them that they are largely unaware of how they participate in getting off track. Events do not force. Reactions force.

To better see the part we play in sabotaging our purpose, we might start by making a record of everything that upsets us as we go through the day—small upsets and large. For example, we can be certain that whenever we become irritated or annoyed, we have forgotten our goal for the day. Something just threw us off track. What specifically was it?

Since at first glance it appears that an event caused the lapse, we record the event. Soon we will look at the events again and differentiate between what happened and our reaction, but for now it's good to assess just how often we lose our hold on happiness in a single day.

During your morning period of preparation you will reach a certain level of happiness, which of course may vary from morning to morning. Use this level as your guide for the day and note any circumstance during which you fall below it. Is it in rushing to get to an appointment? Is it in the letdown after making a purchase? Is it during a disagreement with a friend? Is it while on the phone with a relative?

After several days of taking inventory of what upsets you, you are now ready to look for the pattern behind these upsets. In an attempt to avoid responsibility, we try to perceive every difficulty as uniquely caused. We think we plainly see a new person to blame or a special set of circumstances to justify our reaction. Yet seeing these does not exclude the possibility that our pattern of participation is the same.

Obviously we need to take responsibility for our patterns. It should be noted, however, that responsibility does not mean guilt. Guilt is an inefficient reaction, yet indulging in it is not without consequences. Guilt blocks insight by focusing our attention on ourselves and excluding the people we affected. Unless it is a deeply felt remorse for what we have caused and a strong determination to undo the damage, guilt is just another form of self-indulgence, which is probably what caused the harm in the first place.

In looking over in one sitting the list of upsets that have occurred over several days, the pattern of our involvement can often be seen within the similarity of emotions that we felt throughout this diversity of events. Let's say that the pattern we are not yet seeing is that we believe we are always a victim. As we review recent upsets—for instance, in our marriage, at work, with one of our parents, and while shopping for clothes— maybe we notice a sort of sad, depressed feeling that accompanied most of the upsets. We now focus on this little complex of emotions and ask ourselves, "What does this feeling remind me of? When have I felt this before?" These questions in turn bring to mind other difficult situations from weeks ago, years ago, and sometimes even from our childhood.

Now we are alert to this feeling, and as we go about our life we notice it well up within us again and again. What is this feeling saying? If we were to put it into words, what would those words be? By looking at it carefully each time it comes up, gradually its meaning becomes clear—not because we have guessed what it is but because we have seen what it is. The process I am speaking of is not a play of ideas or an intellectual exercise. It is passionless observation. What emotion drives these upsets, and what thought drives the emotion?

Perhaps the meaning of the sad depression is seen to be "I think I am always a victim. I think everything that happens to me that I don't like is someone else's fault." Or let's say that as we review our list of upsets, the dominant emotion we see is not depression but anger. Therefore we ask, "What does this anger remind me of? What does it symbolize? What is it saying?" And again, we are alert to it in new situations that we find difficult until at last we are able to put it into words— "Life has not treated me fairly, and you are going to pay for it." Or, "The genes I inherited (my last two husbands, the parents I got, the illnesses I've had) were unfair, and I will vent my anger on you."

Notice that the words you put to the underlying feeling are never specific to the various upsetting events. And notice also that they are always essentially the same words.

The upset-generating emotions and what they mean will of course differ with each person. What will not differ is the fact that our unhappiness has a central pattern, and that pattern can be seen if we are willing to look. We are not responsible for what the day brings to us, but we are responsible for reacting to everything in the same miserable way—even if it's only slightly miserable!

Starting at the Top of the Weed

Having identified the pattern of our unhappiness, now comes the problem of shaking loose the pattern. Identifying and removing the pattern of our happiness can be the work of a lifetime, and this book addresses that problem in several ways. Nevertheless, let's consider one possible approach at this time.

As we look at the habitual ways we make ourselves unhappy, there appears to be more than one emotion and thought behind them. Then as we take up the work of loosening the grip of these thoughts and feelings, their number seems to shrink or to consolidate until one central pattern is seen to be at the base of all the others. That insight will occur when it occurs, and nothing is gained by trying to guess what the one pattern is. Nor are those who can cite their core pattern further along spiritually than those who can't. In fact, the entire approach of identifying patterns of unhappiness and removing them will be helpful to some people and not to others. There are millions of roads to happiness, and this is just one of them. But since we have embarked on this one, let's explore it a little further.

Our core emotion and thought produces patterns of outward difficulties, and it's natural for us to want to eliminate these symptoms more than we want to tackle their root cause. If we think of our life as a garden, in my opinion it's better to begin by lopping off the top of the weeds than attempting to dig up their roots. If we can see that our garden can at least appear to be weed-free, we are greatly encouraged. The downside of course is that new patterns of difficulties soon surface and our work begins all over again.

Another illustration of the tops-of-the-weed approach can be seen in the way many people deal with alcoholism, which is a pattern of outward behavior with a root cause. Many alcoholics who learn how to stop drinking are observed by others to still have the personality of an alcoholic. True, the root cause has not been eliminated, but would anyone argue that the individual has made no gains by eliminating drunkenness?

Let's say that your core emotion and thought is manifesting itself in an inability to keep a job, or maintain your weight, or sustain a romantic relationship, or complete tasks, or drive without getting angry. If you have kept a record of your moments of upset over several days, you have surely run across one or two behavioral patterns that you would like to be done with. Pick one of the minor patterns and try the following:

- First calm your mind and body and rest a moment in comfort. Now look honestly at the pattern of behavior and acknowledge that this is something you have a problem with. For example, say to yourself, "I frequently arrive late. I arrive late at work, at parties, for appointments, and so on."

- Then ask yourself, "Does my pattern of arriving late make me happy?"

- Next ask, "Is there something I want to do about this? Am I willing to make an effort?"

- In conclusion ask, "What might I try that would have a chance of making things better?"

Do not attempt to come up with an answer that will dissolve the pattern perfectly and forever. All you want is one measure that would make it easier for you to remain happy. It doesn't matter whether the measure is mental or physical, but it does matter that you not limit your options when deciding what steps to take.

If it would help to begin by listing some totally absurd solutions in order to loosen your thoughts, then by all means use this trick or any other that helps you not be narrow-minded.

Consider the silly as well as the practical steps.

> "If I lived on an iceberg, I would never be late."

> "If I left for an appointment the day before, I would never be late."

> "If I honestly calculated the time it would take to arrive and added 10 percent, I might seldom be late."

> "If as a symbol of my devotion to the Divine, I lived by the rule that I always arrive 5 minutes early, I might seldom be late."

> "If I concentrated on the feelings of the person who has to wait for me, I might seldom be late."

Any pattern, however chronic, is finite, and only a finite number of steps are needed to walk past it. If you persist, the day must come when this pattern, whatever it is, will be behind you. Either it will no longer matter or it will be solved in practical terms.

This is a gentle process. Try it happily. Only happiness leads to happiness. Avoid anxiously casting about for solutions. The mind is of little use when it jumps around. Avoid throwing up your hands in defeat if something you try doesn't work. Often a good solution has several components. If something you try helps a little, keep it as part of the overall solution, then add something else.

CHAPTER

8

SIDE ROADS

The Ego's Use of Goals

The great common door through which most forms of negativity enter the mind is premature expectation. If we watch our thoughts carefully, we see that from the moment we get out of bed, we start deciding how each minor event must work out in order for us to have a "good" day. But as usual the day is perverse and refuses to go along. "I must have Uncle Sam's Cereal" (yet, unknown to us, our spouse has just spooned the last little flaxseed into his or her admittedly cute mouth). "I must have a long soak in the tub" (yet in the middle of it our child calls us to come see the wonderful thing the cat just threw up). "I must leave the house by eight o'clock." "I must drive to work in 25 minutes." "I must get my favorite parking place."

In a downward spiral we carry our frustration from one activity into the next. The only part of the day that's reliable is the nagging sense that somehow life shouldn't be this way.

Even though much can be done in the present, a surprising amount of our frustration is over what we can't possibly do anything about. It has already happened, or it's something that will never happen, or it may happen but can't be acted on today, or we simply have no control over the event in question.

The habit of going through the day absently setting the terms of our happiness may appear to be a kind of thinking that is different from frustration. Actually, it is only a more focused form of fear, one that is concentrated on the immediate future and therefore seemingly more practical. You swing your feet out of bed and the first thing that catches your attention is your spouse's underpants. "I must mention that," you say to yourself. "This will not be a happy marriage until that stops." (Yet you've been mentioning it for the past twelve years.) Or you notice that the carpet needs vacuuming. "Jeff and Stacy are coming for dinner. I've got to take care of that before I leave for work." (But in rushing to fix your breakfast you drop the last container of vegan egg substitute, and by the time you've cleaned between your toes, not only is there no time left to vacuum, you have to forgo the French toast you had your heart set on.)

Have your heart instead set on peacefully doing whatever you are doing now. Because, remember, nothing will go right today. And if it does, it will only scare you.

The things that truly need to be taken care of will be taken care of if we remain in the present. But we must not incessantly question ourselves about what those things might be, because to do so makes us lean out of the present and become less efficient. More to the point, it makes us unhappy not to do well what we are doing now. We simply carry on with the activity of the moment in the most peaceful way possible, and, as John Wooden says, we strive to make today our masterpiece. Our ability to be happy grows inexorably from repeated attempts to exercise it, despite how unsuccessful we may think we are each time.

Stop occasionally and ask yourself if this is what you want to be doing. At least ask yourself if this is how you want to be feeling. If you are about to begin a new activity, pause and ask yourself if this is what you want to do next. Never be afraid of your heart's preference, because, unlike your ego preference, it will always answer for the present. It will guide you from where you are now and not fill your mind with pointless longings. It is indeed possible to eliminate once and for all the vague feeling that there is somewhere else we would rather be, something else we would rather be doing.

The Ego's Definition of Now

Our ego's idea of staying in the present is to continue doing whatever we are doing at all costs. When operating from this part of ourselves we react irritably to anything that thwarts the pursuit of our immediate goal, even though we have never stopped long enough to see if we believe in the goal. Even a flicker of anger is a reliable signal that we have fallen into this trap. On the other hand, our heart's desire is to do what we are doing happily and well. It is *not* to prevent interruptions.

Why does everything have to be finished? Why is that better? Why does every phone call have to be answered? Every book completed? Every movie and TV drama watched to its depressing conclusion? Every party attended until someone else leaves first? Every attack endured until the last bitter word has been thought of? True happiness is flexible because it's geared to an inner state that can be controlled and not to the world, which never can be. There will always be interruptions, and this must become unimportant.

Unquestionably it's helpful not to be scattered, even though we live in a world that is thoroughly disjointed. It's good to know what our priorities are and resist needlessly jumping from one pursuit to another. For example, if it's important that the house be cleaned, you would not, as you pass by your desk, sit down and start paying bills, because bills are not your priority. However, this doesn't mean that you must finish the countertops before you pick up the living room or that while picking up the living room you shouldn't stop to straighten a picture, since all of this is part of your priority.

But what usually occurs is we think, "This will eventually have to be done, so I might as well do it now." But that category is open-ended. We walk into the bathroom because it's time to get ready for bed, and with the new organically waxed floss dangling from our teeth, we peer wistfully into the mirror hoping for a brighter smile. But all we see is a three-day accumulation of toothpaste splatters. Dutifully we set the floss down and march to the kitchen for the Glass Plus. There we notice that someone has left the milk out. When we open the fridge to put it back, an evil-smelling aroma engulfs us and an hour later we have half the food we own on the floor and we still haven't found what has gone bad. However, we do manage to sponge off the shelves and rearrange all the condiments according to height—once again proving how much humans love to start projects they can't finish just when it's time to sleep.

The Ego's Answer to Conflict

Possibly you can see that by asking yourself if what you are doing is what you want to be doing, you are apt to look more honestly at whether you wish to continue being conflicted. Conflict causes us to be a little late and never to quite complete the things that truly should be completed. So close your eyes and say, "I am balancing the checkbook. This is what I chose to do. If I rush through this trying to get to the TV, there is no way I can be happy now." And, surprisingly, the task is done more quickly despite the time taken for this pause, and it is certainly done more happily.

Barging ahead is the ego's way of resolving conflict. Since our ego is our insane belief that appearances are everything, this tactic seems perfectly logical, for if we are *doing* something, we do not *appear* to be conflicted. Therefore, rush into activity, fill the air with words, peruse a dozen remedies at once if you are sick, busy yourself with something, anything, if you are depressed, but whatever you do, do not rest a moment in peace and consider your heart's desire. Because, to our ego, pausing *appears* to be indecision.

Despite its enormous drain on our energy, tension does not get us what we want. We want to be fully alive now. We want to know wholeness. But how can we know it if we feel conflicted about what we are engaged in? Tension is a signal that we have set a goal that slights the present. If we are under stress, we have assumed that something in the future is more meaningful and that the present is merely a thing that must be gotten through. This is an unhelpful attitude because we are avoiding the one thing we cannot escape: now. The only day we will ever live is the one we call today, and the one lesson worth learning is how to walk through today in peace.

Starting with the period just after your morning quiet time and continuing on through to the start of your mental preparation for sleep, look carefully at how your day usually goes. What are the low points, and when is the lowest point of all?

So far we have been attempting to become more conscious of upsets, especially recurring upsets. Now we want to observe how these are regularly grouped within a single day. For example, it's quite common for there to be a series of small annoyances and frustrations every morning. Most people are not reasonable in how they start the day. They have never sat down and worked out an intelligent morning schedule. Consequently they are always caught off guard by *something* and begin the day in confusion, behind time, slighting their own body's needs and often running roughshod over other people's feelings. Even if they have had an early meditation, they end up throwing away most of their stability because for them morning is not a time but a transition.

Once we begin to see that there are predictable periods when most of our setbacks occur and that there are other times when very little upsets us, we see that we are not so much a victim of circumstances as we are of moods. This allows us to discover ways to avoid the moods that cause the setbacks.

Starting the Day Over

Even though the graph of each person's vulnerability to upset varies, sometimes so sharply that there are occasionally true "morning people" and "night people," for most of us little discouragements accumulate as the day progresses. Usually by late afternoon our minds are distracted and more susceptible to unhappy emotions. This dynamic is avoidable, and a routine that anticipates it can be helpful.

Take what you believe to be the lowest period of your day and schedule a small break just prior to it. If your job or other circumstances make this awkward, plan it as close to your time of vulnerability as possible. If from, say, three o'clock on you are typically grumpy and tired, and if it's not feasible for you to stop at two or two-thirty, perhaps you could set aside a few minutes around lunchtime.

How easily you are able to schedule this and how consistently you remember to do it will depend of course on how important happiness is to you. It's good to be clear that misery has benefits and payoffs. Choosing darkness provides us with a set of pleasures, and these need to be looked at. If year after year you are irritable in the late afternoon, obviously you see some benefit in being this way. For example, perhaps you feel more justified in saying some hurtful things that you have wanted to say. Perhaps you can make certain people tiptoe around you. Perhaps you can indulge your cynicism and wallow a little in the thought that nothing really matters. Perhaps your shift in mood allows you to get out of doing a few things you would rather not do.

However, if you are clear that you want to break with your habitual letdown, a good way to start might be to close your eyes and mentally divide the day into two days. Declare the old day over and done with and the new day beginning as of now. Perhaps look at your watch to mark the time. Be firm with yourself that your purpose is to let go of the things that have already occurred. Recall your purpose for the day and set it again as if for the first time.

You may need to give some incident special attention in order to let it go. If so, here is a visualization you might try:

Picture, one at a time, the people involved in what happened and mentally surround each one in light. Do this until you feel your grip on what you are holding onto loosen a little. If the incident involved only you, picture yourself once again going through it, only this time surrounded in light.

An unconflicted motive heals the mind. That is why doing something as uncomplicated as surrounding in light is often all that's needed. If on occasion you want a more thorough procedure, you might try surrounding in light not only the people who were involved in the disturbing incident but also every object in the scene. See each separate thing you focus on as innocent. Say,

"That is just a chair. It is completely innocent."

"That is just a phone. It is completely innocent."

"Those are only the eyes of a face. They are completely innocent."

Do this with anything in the scene that catches your attention as you review it.

Some people find that doing something physical releases the usual mood more effectively. If so, the following are a few possibilities.

- Sit it on the edge of a chair and lean forward, letting your arms and head dangle toward the floor. Slumped forward and totally relaxed, feel everything that happened to you earlier "roll off your back" and drain completely from you.

- Or slowly drink a glass of water, and as you take each sip, picture the water cleansing you of all accumulated defeats.

- Or walk quickly for a moderate distance or up a flight of stairs, and as you walk, feel yourself leaving completely behind the "old" day. This has the added benefit of gearing up the metabolism, an effect that can last for an hour or two.

The Positive Use of Doubt

It's often said that we can forgive but we can't forget. Yet to forgive in a way that restores our happiness, we must relinquish our desire to recall, and this is decidedly not a hopeless task. An idea, image, or desire is relinquished once it is recognized as meaningless within the present. Imagine the private lines of thought that might follow a network announcement that, after a close count, a particular candidate for president had won and how dramatically those thoughts would shift if later the nation learned that another candidate had assumed office. Many people experienced precisely this turnabout in thinking during the 2000 presidential election. But who continued pursuing thoughts of what all it meant to have Gore as our new president once Bush was in office? The original premise had become meaningless within the present. So let's consider a little more fully why it is equally meaningless to harbor a grievance about what someone did.

This much should be clear: We will not know peace while using our mind to attack. Even if the attack is against ourself. When the mind focuses on a failing, including an imagined failing, it is imbued with the sadness of that subject. There is no joy in perceiving another's weakness, although our ego argues that the comparison is good for it. Indeed our ego, or sense of separateness, lives off the blood of these comparisons. Yet contrary to this unhappy attitude, the *experience* of seeking out and treasuring guilt is consistently miserable. We continue seeking it because, sadly, we carry the hope that next time the darkness we pinpoint in another will add light to us, even though this kind of boost to our self-esteem has always collapsed after a short while.

Our ego can, and often does, use its own version of forgiveness as a way of attacking still further. We may approach the person directly and in effect say, "I want you to know that although it wasn't easy, I have finally forgiven you for what you did." Or we may carry on the attack mentally: "Surely God will forgive him—perhaps in two thousand years?" We may even explain to ourselves *why* the person did what he did, but we never question our impression of *what* he did. Yet it is the "what" that must be let go of if our mind is to be free of pain.

Grievances arise from not having all the facts. As has been

well said, "To understand all is to forgive all," but it doesn't follow that the answer is to increase our understanding, because no matter how much we increase it, we still will not understand *all*.

Perhaps the preliminary insight is this: *To see our perfect ignorance is to exonerate others from imperfection.* To say, "I do not know" releases us from feelings of separateness. When we acknowledge that the grounds for our point of view may be faulty or distorted, we begin relinquishing that point of view. Blame simply cannot be established in any final sense. Nor can innocence be effectively *argued*. The sane approach is to stop thinking about what others have done instead of trying to "understand" why they did it.

If we have a strong personal opinion about anything, we are wrong. The only real issue is happiness. If we are making others happy, we are right—not of course if we're only appeasing their egos, but truly adding to their peace. If we are making them unhappy, we are wrong. And our treasured opinions never make anyone happy, not in the deep, restful sense of that word. The one stand to take is peace—firmly being it and consistently extending it. Any stand that does not offer genuine peace to another is not justified, and will never be justified, no matter how many people we get to say they agree with us. We all do the best we can, and herein lies our innocence. What more do we need to "understand" than this?

To forgive is to turn away from the past out of a strong interest in the present. This is what young children do so easily. They are not more virtuous, they are simply more interested in playing with their friends now than in dwelling on what they did 10 minutes ago. As adults we have logic to aid us. We admit that we are not qualified, and thus we are incapable of judging. For indeed this is a fact. "Who am I to judge?" points to a miraculous truth that should be guarded like an antidote to poisoning. Sit quietly and say, "What happened is not worth thinking about because it is beyond me to understand it perfectly. I therefore choose not to dwell on it. And because I am sincere, I am willing to do whatever is needed to drop it."

This approach does not trivialize any damage that may have been inflicted in the past. The truth is many of us have suffered greatly at the hands of others. Nor does it ask you to reinterpret events. Rather, it is an approach that allows you to heal the mind, where the effects of the damage reside. At some time a choice must be made about whether we wish to remain living proof of all that has been done to us, or whether we would rather emerge from the ashes of the past.

Breaking with the Situation

All judgmental thoughts come into our mind in the context of a situation. Our body is doing something at the time our mind darkens, and seldom is the connection between negative thinking and what we are doing apparent. Nor does any connection have to be seen. But regardless of our activity, we do need to notice that we have just lost our happiness.

When John and Jordan were still quite young, all four of us were diagnosed by their pediatrician as having a systemic yeast infection. Under her supervision we began taking Nystatin. After about three weeks of strictly following the pediatrician's instructions on diet and medication, I suddenly began to remember how I had felt many years ago. I felt good. I was alert. I was full of energy. I no longer needed naps. I could play with the boys without getting exhausted.

What struck me as odd was that until I started feeling good, I did not realize I had felt bad. My energy level had not seemed low, needing naps had not seemed unusual. Now I had no desire ever to return to that "normal" state again. And being happy—even though it is a spiritual state, not a physical one—

is similar. We have to know some measure of peace and happiness in order to appreciate what we are missing during those times we suffer their absence. This is why establishing a baseline of happiness in the morning can be helpful.

Once this habit is in place, another habit can be added to protect our mental wholeness. We can begin practicing "breaking from the situation," which means momentarily stopping what we are doing the instant we realize that we are experiencing a loss of peace. This may entail getting up from the table, sitting down in the mall, excusing ourself from a conversation, or merely putting the paring knife down and standing in the kitchen a moment with our eyes closed.

The instant you recognize that you are less than happy, do something to symbolize to yourself that there is something more important than the worldly activity you are engaged in, and that one thing is your state of mind. Perhaps this new habit I am suggesting seems radical to you. "Radical" means what goes to the root. So, yes, this step is radical.

Few people realize how important symbols are when attempting to reestablish communication with their own mind. Our bodily actions keep our mind informed of our true priorities. If you see that you are not happy yet continue right on with what you are doing, your mind will resist any tampering with its confusion. But if, for example, you pull your car off the road, call for quiet, and talk directly to your mind, what is said gets through now because you have your own attention. A recognizable gain in serenity is the result, not because sitting, closing eyes, and other such activities are somehow "good," but because for most of us they are strong symbols, just as for example dropping to one's knees in prayer is a powerful symbol in some religions.

If you had diarrhea you would break with almost anything. Is your happiness as important as diarrhea? What are you willing to *do* to bring peace to your life? If you had diarrhea you would let the phone ring, you would give up your place in the checkout line, you would not answer the front door, you would miss the end of the movie, you would interrupt your breakfast and let your toast return to room temperature. But what are you prepared to do if you lose your peace?

Before you will ever know what it feels like to go through just one day totally unafraid and completely happy, you must first be willing to look honestly at all the things you currently put before your need for a consistent mental state: Needing to be on time? Needing to interrupt and make your point? Wanting "to get ahead" in business, on the highway, and perhaps even in play? Having to pursue a sexual object? Dreading to offend? The list goes on and on, but the truth is that no room exists in most people's lives for a different kind of priority, especially one so gentle as happiness.

And what do you do once you have broken with the situation? Surprisingly enough, it really doesn't matter, as long as you think in some calming way. So perhaps you talk to yourself from the heart and remind yourself what is truly important. Or you recall a line from scripture. Or you take several slow deep breaths. Or you are still and blank for a moment so that you can settle down and "come to your senses."

Not much time is needed. You may be surprised to discover that your sudden absence from a social situation is rarely commented on or even noticed. Expressions such as "Hold on a minute" and "I'll be right back" are so often heard that almost no one pays attention to them or to the sudden departures that follow. The ancient needs of bowels and bladders have already paved your way for many unsuspected meditations.

Entire days are frequently lost to confusion, discouragement, resentment, jealousy, bitterness, or other versions of unhappiness only because one small stirring of the ego was neglected and grew into an engulfing mood. Breaking with the situation is a reliable way of quickly restoring your peace and happiness. And it is simple enough to use for a lifetime.

CHAPTER

9

LETTING GO

The Weight of the Past

Many people see the relevance of starting the day with a sound orientation and of following a reasonable plan for dealing with habitual patterns of daily distress. Yet it may not be obvious why getting ready for bed is important enough to merit its own chapter. Everyone knows you just brush your teeth, put on your Snoopy nightshirt, pull up the covers, and turn off the light.

It is not an overstatement to say that if at the end of the day we prepared our mind spiritually for sleep, we would eventually master all the rules of happiness. There is of course no reason to confine ourselves to this one form of effort, but the manner in which we fall asleep is so filled with spiritual potential that it could truly be considered a yoga or "way" of happiness.

The means of unhappiness are the accumulation and retention of a past. One reason that young children are so noticeably happy and have such impossible energy is that they drag very little past behind them. They come into the world unencumbered by experience and free of anxiety about the implications of what has already occurred. It's difficult to get most two-, three-, and four-year-olds to answer any questions at all about what they did while we weren't with them. They are so interested in what's happening now that the past is an obvious bore in comparison.

At the preschool John attended when he was two and three, there was always an afternoon snack prepared by a rotating list of parents, which the teachers and all the kids would sit down and eat together. In those days Gayle and I were concerned that John was not eating enough, so after picking him up from school we would not only inspect the almost untouched contents of his lunch box but would also casually ask what the snack had been that day, hoping to discover whether he had at least eaten *that*. The first few weeks he simply said he didn't know, but when he saw that this didn't put an end to it, he began answering, "Noodles." And "noodles" it remained until we realized that he had such little interest in the subject that he probably did not remember.

Children are gradually taught to carry the past with them by questions like these, and even to fear it by such warnings as "Don't do that. Remember what happened last time?" By their teens or early twenties, and sometimes much sooner, a mental turnabout occurs, and the past is thereafter put above the present as their main concern.

The life goals of most adults are motivated by the fantasy that their "accomplishments" will become a "permanent" part of their past and therefore of themselves. Our usual assumption is that our identity is everything we have done and not how we are this instant. That is why many people find it difficult to complete a personal transformation while remaining in close contact with those who have known them all their lives. Often our old acquaintances just can't see that we are truly changing. They are convinced we are the same, and so they get angry or suspicious when we don't respond the way we always have.

Our fear of mistakes also comes from the assumption that our past behavior is more real than our present mental state. Whatever error we commit is incorporated into our identity, remaining plainly within our history for all to see—never a correctable mistake, always an abiding sin. Inevitably there is a mishap or lapse or personal failure, and from that point on we are a recovering alcoholic, ex-mental patient, or convicted shoplifter. Our insurance premiums are high because once we had a wreck. We still have difficulty getting a loan because of the time we were unable to meet our bills. After my first book was published, one newspaper ran a story on me headlined "Ex-Real Estate Broker in the Tradition of Rod McKuen" because of a job I had in my early twenties.

In light of the honor it pays the past, all these correlations appear reasonable, for how could one rightly praise past accomplishments without also cherishing guilt? Yet emphasis on the past produces fear of the present. That much should be obvious. However, what is often not recognized is that all forms of fear transport psychological *weight* into the present.

There is no such thing as "idle" worry. Worries don't idle; they grind. Fear presses upon the body as well as on the mind. By the time most of us reach the so-called golden years—the culmination of our efforts to build the best past we could—we have become so weighed down with all the miserable lessons we carry with us that we are in permanent depression and despair, as a visit to almost any home for the elderly shows. There are individuals who escape this, but it's not by accident.

Another showcase of worldly happiness, the romantic

relationship, breaks up or enters a stage of repressed futility when the *history* of the relationship becomes all that the two people can see in each other. Once again, very few escape this. One can walk into a restaurant and with surprising accuracy pick out the "old" married couples by the noticeable lack of love between them. I am sure you have had the experience of hearing people you know well talk about their spouse, then on meeting and getting to know that person discovered that they were blind to many of their partner's good qualities. The reason you could see their spouse more accurately than they was that to a large degree you had no choice but to see that individual from the present.

People are never now how they have always been. Even though the amount varies, some growth and flowering is occurring in each life.

Our perceived defeats weigh us down, yet what we think of as our victories can be equally smothering. For example, life can become very difficult for those who had great physical beauty when they were young. And a body can appear to be a curse when its athletic gifts are spent. Past presidents of major corporations, former politicians, old actors and singers know well the feeling of being looked at as if they are freaks. For us to succeed, someone must fail. Once worldly success is ours, we are not suddenly exempt from the social dynamic that brought it.

To have a hold on us this misery must be mentally reentered daily, and the doorway we provide is our preoccupation with what happened. There is very little that can hurt you once you learn how to release your mind from what you accumulated mentally during the day.

Releasing Residue

The process of taking on the weight of the past is unmistakable even in the course of a few hours. Very early in the day something fails to go as expected, and a slight discouragement is carried unnoticed into the next activity. As a consequence, the new activity is not performed satisfactorily, and an additional worry is set silently into place. As the day progresses, a mounting sense of bleakness and weariness becomes unavoidable, all of which is so noticeably absent in young children because their reigning interest in the present allows them to dismiss each event at its close.

A state of mind this simple can't be recaptured at once, but it can be attained deliberately. To this end there are three tools that can be helpful. One is the kind of break we discussed before that one schedules into the course of the day. Another is the pause between events discussed in chapter 4. The third is a major period of relinquishment at the close of the day.

The methods you use to clear your mind are not critical, but how unconflicted you are about wanting to is. If you truly wish to let go of the past, you will find ways to accomplish this. When you sit down to commence one of these practices, if you are not clear about its purpose or satisfied that it is all you want to pursue for the next few moments, what technique you use or how long you engage in it will matter very little. You simply won't achieve meaningful results.

So the first rule of relinquishment is to be certain you know what you are about to attempt and why it is important to you. Then begin using one of the methods described in this book or something else you have found useful, and when the day comes that you feel its effectiveness starting to wane, do not hesitate to try another technique. All remedies eventually lose their efficiency because, to some degree, trust has been placed in mere method. Do not let this fact discourage you. The number of approaches still available will be too numerous to exhaust.

When John was five and Jordan was two, we all used to gather on the king-size bed and let go of the day by picturing a rocket. (Before that we pictured a hot-air balloon, but it took too long to get it out of sight). This was a special rocket containing an electromagnetic time capsule (you succumb to this kind of talk when you have a five-year-old boy). With our eyes closed, we silently went back over the day and imagined anything that was still burdening us being dumped into the time capsule (mistakes, regrets, embarrassments, grudges, excitements, as well as fears or longings about the future). After we emptied ourselves of every scene or person that was cluttering our thought, we switched on the magnetic force of the time capsule and imagined it drawing out of us anything we missed. During this final purging process we counted down from 10 to blast-off.

I'm not sure where Gayle sent her rocket. I aimed mine into a black hole, never to be heard from again. If one of the concerns I released was something that would need attention in the future, I sent that worry into high orbit where I couldn't see it but could get it back when the time came for me to act on it. We have a friend who suggests a simpler approach: Imagining putting these bits of unfinished business on a line out of sight, then hauling them in the next day when you have a moment to devote to them.

The object is to lift everything from your mind that is of no use to you now that you are going to sleep. The side benefit is that the ego is lessened in the process. A surprising number of our unhappy personal experiences reappear in the form of reactions within any given day. To relinquish the day is also to let go of a portion of the ego itself and thus make a small but permanent gain in happiness. It is precisely because of this side effect that the practice of letting go of the day is so profound.

Techniques of Release

Schedule your period of relinquishment as close as you can to the time you will fall asleep, and try not to do anything that might agitate you afterward (phone calls, watching news, making plans, arguing). Unless of course you are bedridden, it is better not to attempt this process while lying down, because your concentration will tend to be divided. Three or four minutes will often suffice, but there may be days when more time can be well used.

Quietly review the day, then make the conscious effort to let go of anything that is the least bit disturbing. You needn't expect to achieve perfect release, but it's always possible to attain a reassuring sense that you have been thorough.

Along with the letting go exercises already mentioned, here are four other possibilities.

1. Picture *as you* someone for whom you have great respect reenacting the incident you are attempting to release or, if you like, going through the entire day. See yourself back in the same circumstances but as some dear friend, as a loving relative from your childhood, as a being of light, as Jesus, as a saint, or whoever else symbolizes purity and innocence to you. Do not ask yourself how this other person would have *behaved*, but merely think of yourself possessing this individual's perfect gentleness while you imagine going through the incident again. Look through your guide's eyes of peace, feel your guide's acceptance and tolerance, then allow yourself simply to see what happens this time through.

2. Hold in your mind the individual who has done something that disturbs you and pretend that you can now see all that this person has gone through since birth. Allow

yourself to imagine the kinds of circumstances that he or she had to endure at home, at school, and so forth that would explain the behavior and make it completely understandable. Do not try to discover the facts or kid yourself that you can guess them, but merely relax and have a fantasy of what *could* have happened that would make the way he or she acted inevitable.

3. See the individual standing before you, and in your own way silently bless this person. Or if you prefer, choose from the following statements:

"My ego is no better than yours."

"You merely made a mistake. I forgive you out of love of what you will become."

"This is truly not important. In a hundred years there will be no one who even remembers it."

"In your heart lies the innocence of the child you once were."

"I want a peaceful mind more than I want this grievance."

"I would rather be happy than right."

4. My grandmother had a way of releasing difficulties that I looked down on as an adolescent but now appreciate and frequently use myself. There were many tragedies in her long life, and whenever I would see her during one of these periods she would often appear completely unaffected. I would ask her how she was doing, knowing all too well the answer. As always she would say, "I'm not worrying about it. I've turned it over to God."

Be certain that you don't try to explain away what others have done or try to reinterpret their behavior in some insincere way. Mental release doesn't come from seeing that what the other person did is somehow okay. It comes from recognizing that attack thoughts are impractical. They make the mental atmosphere in which we dwell chafing and hostile. Nor is our aim to shift the blame back on ourself. During this concluding meditation of the day we wish to restore the mind to a gentle state regardless of what we, this individual, or anyone else has done. We wish to construct a genuine place of peace where we can now take our rest from all the day's stresses. One sure way to do this is to empty our mind so completely that ease and freedom are the only residue.

Sleep Difficulties

Although insomnia perhaps leads the list, there are any number of sleep problems that plague the average person: restlessness, indigestion, itchy skin, fear of the dark, muscle cramps, recurring dreams, night sweats, oversleeping, grinding one's teeth, and so forth. This is not surprising since most people are habitually conflicted about sleeping. Often there is a lingering sense of tasks unfinished or a vague feeling of some moral responsibility going neglected. With others the fear is more general: a growing realization, now that one more wasted day is passing into night, that the dreams they had for their life will never be realized. So as the hour approaches to get some sleep, the nagging feeling arises that some nebulous something should be set right, that it's not fair to sleep when there is work to be done.

More often the person is not aware of these thoughts but merely feels a little uncomfortable and begins futzing and puttering and once again not getting to bed on time. Notice that the delay is not even devoted to what most needs to be taken care of. It is just more waste added to a day of waste.

Whenever there is a pattern of being late you can be sure

you are conflicted about what you are doing. As with sleep, the answer is not necessarily to eliminate the activity but to become clear about what you want to do. You do not wish to take these formless fears into your sleep, and it's unnecessary to do so.

After you have let the day go and have released your mind from all cares as best you can, take a moment to see that your sole purpose from now until tomorrow morning is to rest both mind and body—and that you have no second purpose. Tell your mind that it is now off duty and there is nothing further you wish it to engage in. Resolve to gently bring your thoughts back to a peaceful idea or fantasy every time they wander into some disquieting consideration. Decide that you will not concern yourself with what you can do nothing about, for there is one good thing you *can* do, and that is to rest.

Time is a luxury, so if it is feasible, be lavish with the time you provide yourself for getting ready for bed, for repose, and for your morning tasks. Unless circumstances make this impossible, do not crowd yourself on either end. While in bed your aim should be to rest your *mind*, and not to force your body to sleep. You wish no war of any sort. Your nights can be enjoyable, and they will be if you concern yourself with what you can accomplish, which is to rest your mind by using it more peacefully.

You are not wiser in the middle of the night than you will be in the morning. You will not make sound decisions about the future if at the moment you want to do two things at once— rest *and* worry. Should you suddenly think of something that will soon require attention, if you need to, put out a reminder, but do not engage your mind in the problem.

If you see that you have begun a disturbing line of thought, do not complete it. Simply interrupt it, and gently, without self-censure, return your attention to more relaxing pursuits. Think about something that will not stir you up. Any thought that contains love has a calming effect. So think about the funny things your children have done. Or imagine yourself gardening if that is what you love. Remember the antics of a pet. Or picture yourself in some wonderful spot where you would love the present and would easily have no cares.

Be sure not to limit yourself. Anything, mental or physical, that you find restful is perfectly all right. Some people find sexual fantasies restful, and there is certainly no harm in these images. Others like to think what they would do if they suddenly came into a great deal of money. Still others find it restful to think about what they would eat if there were no consequences. These subject matters are not traditionally spiritual, but your purpose here is not to stay within some celestially correct list of thoughts. Your purpose is to rest your mind. So what, then, rests it?

Perhaps you would enjoy silently saying a mantra, an affirmation, or some comforting words that come to you at the moment. One chant that I have sometimes repeated is "All released; all is peace." I don't usually think these words in time with my breathing, but when I do I say the first part as I exhale, thinking of anything at all I need to release, and as I inhale I say the second part and breathe in peace. An application that I find useful is to slowly list the people or circumstances that may still be bothering me. For example:

"I release my car; and all is peace."

"I release you (name); and all is peace."

"I release my (stomach, hair, back, nose—whatever part of my body is troubling or embarrassing); and all is peace."

"I release (name of politician or public figure); and all is peace."

"I release my life; and all is peace."

I personally like to think in devotional terms, and this is especially true at night when I am falling asleep. I know that some readers will share this sentiment, so here are several personal examples of a more religious approach.

"I drown in God, and breathe in peace."

"I release the world, and dissolve in God." (I picture myself dropping from the world into a sea of light.)

"The world has been answered. I can go to sleep now."

"Don't be afraid, little mind. Be still. Be calm. Let go now and rest in peace."

"There's no place to go. There's nothing to do. God is with me, and all is well."

Because the newsbreaks and many of the ads and programs on TV appeal strongly to the ego (justified anger, acquisitiveness, fantasies of revenge, physical specialness, tragedy), most television fare can be agitating on an unconscious level and is probably not the best way to get back to sleep or even to "unwind" before going to bed. Television tends to set the wrong life purpose as well as very subtly stir up the body. For most people, there are happier alternatives.

For instance, more control can be exercised over books. It is possible to discover many authors who can be relied on not to jar their readers, and some people find that if they are unable to sleep, reading a little while in a book that is gentle to its characters will often settle their mind to the point where they can sleep. Even if this is not the outcome, it provides them with an alternative way of resting.

I have no idea where I picked up such a silly idea, but for most of my life I would not allow myself to read anything that was not edifying. Reading gradually got to be such an unpleasant activity that the day came when I realized that I had not read a new book of any kind for more than four years. Gayle, on the other hand, finished a new English mystery every three or four days, a practice I not so silently looked down on. But now it was inescapable that although she had "bad reading habits," I had none. I was a self-made illiterate in a world that abounded with good books.

One day I casually asked her if she had read anything that she thought I might *enjoy*. She said maybe I would like the James Herriot books. She was right. So at age forty-five I discovered, for the first time in my adult life, the sheer pleasure of reading, and I now read more books in one year than I had read before in twenty. But for all that, I can no longer drop titles at sophisticated parties. Most people are not impressed with my literary references to Karl Hiaasen and Georgette Heyer. They smile painfully and head for the Brie and smoked salmon on the other side of the room, which, as it turns out, allows me to leave all the earlier and pick up *The Reluctant Widow* where I left off.

Rigid rules, like mine about edifying books, are blind to present needs and do not make happy. For some people, TV, even violent TV, is restful. I also know many adolescents and young adults who find even absurdly violent video and Internet games funny and releasing. For them, these pastimes dissipate anger and tension, and because they are fantasies, they harm no one. The only rule that serves our happiness is the one that serves the present situation. Behavioral guides can be useful, but only as long as they are tentative. The present must be treated seriously if we are to remain reliably kind. And there is no happiness without kindness, whether it is kindness to our body, our mind, or to those around us.

One final exercise that I sometimes find restful is to list every sensation, thought, and emotion I am aware of, and there are of course hundreds of these available. If I am having an especially difficult time keeping my mind in the present, I may even number these as I go along: #1, the dog's snoring; #2, the pull of the sheet against my neck; #3, a passing thought about full moons; #4, something mumbling in my stomach; #5, the cry of a night hawk diving for insects; #6, a quickly dismissed question about the protein content of bugs...

A common refinement of this exercise is to watch the body breathe without attempting to change it. Or to imagine God or the universe filling and emptying our lungs. The reason this type of practice works is that agitation, anxiety, stress, and other unhappy emotions require a past and future in which to operate. Remove these by resting the mind within the present, and mental tranquility is almost automatic. Peace is the very fabric of the mind and therefore its natural state.

Let me reiterate that the mistake most people make when trying to deal with a sleep problem is that they panic, look around for something to blame, and start a mental battle with their sheet-hogging spouse, the clock, their child who needs attending during the night, their pillow, or last night's cooking. Obviously it does not follow that one should never try light stretching, Advil plus a short soak in a warm bath, a truly boring book, a glass of warm milk and honey, herbal teas, a late-afternoon exercise period, a consultation with an authority, or any other simple external remedy about which there is no strong personal fear. To assume greater responsibility for one's body, especially when this is unhurried and unforced, makes any bodily problem simpler. A calm and intelligent willingness to try things is a part of responsibility.

As many have said, it is not helpful to fight yourself. To put this another way: Never deal directly with the ego—yours or anyone else's. For you will merely strengthen it by increasing your belief in its autonomy. Children do not get rid of their imaginary playmates by cursing them. What is imaginary leaves when what is real becomes more interesting. Our ego (our imaginary identity) is best seen clearly, then left behind. It is merely a place of no peace, and to start a slugging match with it always strengthens its hold on our mind. We don't have to quickly do something because we feel a pang of jealousy, depression, fear, or sadness. We simply begin turning from discord to harmony in some restful way. We merely take one or two steps in the direction of the restful side of our mind.

The How and When of Waking Up

The final part of our brief preparation for sleep may be to decide how we will wake up. Most people decide when, but very few decide how. Yet it is how we live our life and not what activities and people it consists of that determines the depth of our enjoyment. Once this is understood, our need to be always changing things begins to dissolve.

Often it's not good to wait until morning to choose how we will awake. During sleep the mind enters an almost pure ego state. In a sense, sleep is dreams about a dream. It is twice removed from reality. That is why it often takes an effort to shift into our saner mental regions, but this can be made easier by knowing in advance what the first thing is we plan to do with our mind.

We have already covered several possible forms our first efforts might take, but what I want to stress here is that because of the dominance of the ego during sleep, our purpose is already set. We must reset it if we wish to avoid taking into our day the same conflicting values that we had in our dreams. Obviously there can be moments of insight and sanity during sleep, and occasionally these are so powerful that the mind wakes in a lifted state. However, these moments are not as frequent as many people like to believe. Yet this belief is not without consequences, because it tends to deny the negative momentum that the mind has built up by morning. This is not something to either fear or fight. Simply notice that a question about a dream, once taken up, never comes *completely* to rest. Therefore, be questionless. Do not waste time trying to understand. Turn instead to the light of happiness so that it will be light rather than questions that you carry with you into the day.

As I stressed earlier, in all endeavors, including repose, try hard and expect very little of yourself. The world attempts to live the opposite rule, and although it is always undergoing some promising new change, it has never once moved close to happiness. This need not be your lot, for when you focus on the means and not the end, on your effort and not its outcome, on the present and not the future, you quietly shift from slight outer accomplishments to immense inner gain.

CHAPTER

10

JOBS

Cutting Back on Problems

The next four chapters deal with jobs, decisions, money, and possessions. Setting aside our body and relationships, which I discuss at the end of the book, these four topics might be called "typical areas of conflict." You may disagree, but just try making a list of typical areas of conflict. You would need to set aside several hours because your list could extend into the night and out the other end. I realize that jobs, decisions, money, and possessions are quite arbitrary. But think of them as examples, for unless you do you may believe that I have left out several of your favorite problems!

It's not inappropriate to impute favoritism in our choice of problems. We are all collectors, and our personalities are just the display cases. We think, talk, and act problems. Secretly we often see the insanity of other people's choices. But our concerns are "real," and we feel personally attacked should anyone fail to adequately toast our problem du jour. Yet so trivial are most of our cares that it's often impossible to remember what we thought was important only last week. The happiness of an entire family can be shattered by just one argument, yet by the next day no one can agree on the incident that started it all.

Have as few problems as possible. This policy will serve you well. Our ego does need some things to gnaw on, but it doesn't need every size chew stick made. Readers need not add the four areas mentioned to their personal list of worries. It's just fine to love your job, to make decisions easily, to have no money problems to speak of (the ultimate criterion), and not to identify with your possessions. In fact it's quite possible (and a good exercise) to make a thorough list of your problems and to check off a few as no longer of real interest. It surprises many people that this can actually be done.

It's also possible to draw in the boundaries of our concerns. This concept was new to me until a few years ago, but Gayle and I have been working on it with good results. We decided to put limits on our worries. Only our family, its paraphernalia, and our closest friends are now permissible. Things like the economy, other people's religions, the mysterious decision-making process of the city streets department, and Tucson newcomers' tastes in landscaping are now mentally off bounds. We have even given up trying to reform our parents and siblings (at best an act of fantasy), much to their relief.

However, it's good to keep the agitated part of the mind harmlessly engaged. Questions such as what is the most natural dishwasher soap, is our dog gaining too much weight (I say "Yes"), does the cat need a friend, and is there truly an educational institution or employer worthy of our children are legitimate trains of thought—provided we don't get too loud about them. After a few years of team effort, we are happy to report that the mind is very amenable to this form of training.

Therefore, except for the general applications, please don't take the next four chapters too personally, unless of course you already have difficulties in these areas. Perhaps pick through the points presented as you would through a box of assorted chocolates (when everyone has left the room). I hope that most of the concepts discussed are simple enough to use in many areas of your life.

Your Job Reveals Nothing About You

I don't recall how old I was when I discovered that if I answered "Architect" instead of "Fireman" to the question "What do you want to be when you grow up?" I got a more satisfying reaction from adults, and I still remember vague feelings of guilt about not knowing what an architect did. Today, some kids are discovering that "firefighter" receives better marks than "architect" or the like. However, we know one six-year-old living in the Tucson foothills who is quite firm about becoming a "venture capitalist."

All of this is harmless because children seem to enjoy this verbal game as much as adults. But a few years later the same question can be terrifying if teenagers feel pressured to divine what high school specialty or college major will best serve them for the rest of their lives. Most parents know that the young person's distress over this is usually without foundation, since so few of us ended up doing what our education prepared us for. Our children should never be scared into thinking that choosing the "right" occupational specialty is crucial to their future happiness.

Believing that appearances are everything, Western culture naturally concludes, "You are what you do." During our middle span of life the seemingly affable question "What do you do?" really means "Are you somebody?" Perhaps most of us think too much about how to word our answer should some stranger at a party ask us this question, even though if we just took a moment to look at our feelings we would see that we really don't care what a stranger thinks. You would suppose it would be self-evident that a person's means of earning a living reveals only the most superficial and insignificant information about what he or she is, yet the issue of career has become a source of great unhappiness.

It is now generally assumed that anyone is capable of doing anything. All you have to do is "want it bad enough." "Why then," our society asks, "have you settled for work that is mediocre or boring?" We should somehow be more creative, more athletic, more humanitarian, more productive, more prosperous, more something. So tangled up with our job are our feelings of self-worth that businesses, if they want their fair share of good employees, must periodically revise job titles to make the same work sound more impressive.

We have actually gotten to the point of rejecting people for not doing more than they do! We ourselves cannot sidestep the disgust, however mild, we think we have reserved only for others. Surely it doesn't have to be proved that all of this is insane. Yet if we wish to be happy, we must free ourselves from this point of view. We are not what we do; we are how we do it.

Individuals do not think better of themselves by engaging in a selection of activities currently considered to be impressive. Nor do they recognize their worth by avoiding them. You will know that you are good when you consistently bring goodness to all you do. If the job is to straighten and clean for a small family, your work is no less holy than, for instance, that of a personnel manager who hires and fires hundreds of employees for a large corporation.

We have such silly ideas of what is important work! For example, what more far-reaching activity could there be than devoting oneself to helping a child be happy and unafraid and develop into a decent, kind adult? How many people will this one child touch within a lifetime? Is seeing to this young person's happiness really less significant than composing music, designing Web sites, breathing with your tongue in the yogic position, being socially in demand, or living up to your earning potential?

Your Career Forms Behind You

Most people have never stopped to ask themselves exactly what it is they are seeking in place of a good life *now*. There simply is no such thing as a career. People talk about pursuing a career as if all the turns were already mapped out and their destination sat there waiting for them as solid and immovable as the town civic center.

Except for the straight-line promotions within organizations such as the armed services, a few large corporations, and some branches of civil service, none of us advances to our goal with a predictable precision. Even within the fields where this appears to happen, a closer examination shows a nest of entangling exceptions—employees' health and will to endure, exigencies of location, family demands, government allocations, and the goodwill of superiors. It is not realistic to think in terms of "arriving at the top of your profession." There is no perfectly defined profession and no true top.

Our trail through life can be seen only in retrospect. It *does* all add up, but not in advance of the steps taken. If each small step is guided by the present instead of by a hodgepodge of fears about the future, we can discern a lovely wake flowing from the actions we have taken, including our mistakes. There is a beauty and a just-rightness within the course of most people's lives. But so often the individual is blinded to this by constant worry and second-guessing.

The only "career move" you can be certain about is whether you feel at peace in the present about a step that is possible to take today. No one can adequately define all the consequences, see all the people this step will affect, and accurately determine the ramifications in each of these individuals' lives. We merely delude ourselves if we think our vision is that free of distortion. Why then attempt to resolve interminable future implications when it's simply not possible to do so? Instead of the fantasy of a glowing future, why not settle for the very real possibility of a satisfying present?

Nothing Has to Be Decided in Advance

When we attempt to translate a fantasy into a worldly event, the result is a different order of reality. Like most people, I have run through many such fantasies in my life. My mental pictures of what it would be like to be a sculptor, ranch hand, secondary schoolteacher, Christian Science practitioner, real estate broker, guidance counselor, construction worker, circuit lecturer, and a few other false starts were so unlike the reality of the work I ended up engaged in that it's funny to me now that I thought I could see in advance what my life would be like within these fields.

A fantasy does not give firsthand experience. That is why no matter how informed we think we are, we don't know beforehand what will make us happy. Nor is there any reason to know, since it's the degree to which we have developed our capacity to enjoy the present—and not our job classification—that determines our happiness. This doesn't mean that very little care need be taken in choosing one's way of making a living. It means only that our freedom from conflict over whether today to ask for an interview, enroll in a class, question someone within a certain line of work, or buy a book or two on a particular field is a more reliable basis for making a decision than our fantasy of a future course of action that will entail hundreds of separate choices. Our desire to anticipate every move we will make for broad periods of time is nothing more than our present wish to struggle—to struggle to control a future that cannot be controlled. All we need do is take the obvious steps before us today and let our sense of direction clarify as we proceed.

As touched on before, there is also a strong tendency to get ourselves into a difficult situation, then think we must see it through to the bitter end. Trusting in fantasies instead of our present perception is a major contributor to this pattern. To decide beforehand what kind of job we deserve can cause as much unhappiness as deciding what kind of child we have a right to, as many parents unconsciously do. In their mind is a constantly escalating standard of acceptable manners, the proper height, an adequate IQ, sufficient social skills, a pleasing appearance, and so forth. Inevitably the child fails in some respect and feels his parents' disapproval. Disapproval is directly opposed to appreciating children and working with them toward their, rather our own, feelings of well-being. And just as with a child, a job must be looked at in the present, taken as it is, and given time.

Relax into your destiny. Let each workday come to you. Watch it approach without suspicion. Expect happiness from yourself, but expect nothing from the job. Take each task as it comes, and do not peer over it to the next task. Don't rush to complete it or rush toward some hour on the clock. We need not stay on guard to see that a job is not working out and to quit it, but we do have to let down our guard to enjoy what we have predefined as "work." We may not be able to change the task, but we are always free to change our definition of our function within it.

Finding a Job

Our discussion so far may seem insensitive to the many people who sincerely want to work but can't find employment. This is an extremely complex and difficult issue, and the factors within individual cases can vary so dramatically that any generalizations I make here will be unfair in light of at least some people's plight. Although there are countless exceptions, I believe a few things can be said that apply to some of those who find themselves in this predicament.

Many people—far more than consciously realize it—make themselves walk a very narrow path in finding work. For instance, there are entire categories of jobs they won't consider because of a self-image they believe must be maintained. Other occupations go unexplored because of their conviction that society, the economy, the present controlling minority, big business, or some other generalized enemy should not be forcing this kind of choice and they must stand alone against this outrage, even if it means their family's well-being. "I won't work for a company that...."; "I won't live in a place where...."; "I won't take orders from a boss who...."; and yet it does not have to be this way. Clearly we should never do what is morally intolerable, but so often this is not the real issue. We think we must be right at all costs.

Another hampering bias is directed, curiously, at ourselves. Most people tend to look down on what they do best. This is further evidence of our aversion to what is easy and simple. Our areas of greatest strength are usually the ones we designate for the harshest scrutiny. And if we look for fault anywhere long enough, we are sure to find it. Instead of doing what we know how to do (which often is the work we can do most peacefully), we assume that the higher pursuit is to enter a new field altogether, especially one that fits the current definition of "meaningful" work. Seldom is it sufficient to simply earn a living. Better to have an erratic income and be able to give the impression that we are sacrificing ourselves to set the world straight.

The reverse of this attitude is also a hindrance to finding a job and is perhaps even more prevalent. Salary, not job description, is the dominant consideration. People feel insulted or embarrassed at the starting salary of many jobs and opt for no income instead of taking what is available today. Their assumption is that by being out of work entirely they stay in a better position to take advantage of future opportunities. But this discounts the sometimes positive attitudinal effects of doing something.

In thirty years of counseling couples, I have heard the following argument between girlfriend and boyfriend, husband and wife, hundreds of times. First partner: "Isn't some job better than no job?" Second partner: "No. If I'm working at this piddling job you think I should take, I can't interview for the kind of job I could get." Watching these arguments play out over many years, I have noticed that the person who takes a lesser job often ends up with a better job more quickly than the person who waits for the "right" job. No spiritual law is at work here, and sometimes the person who waits is later justified, but I believe that deciding what to do today usually works out better than taking a stand that locks us in to only one option day after day.

Unfortunately our friends are sometimes the ones most likely to distract us from our own quiet knowing. As a general rule, you will be less confused and consequently miss fewer opportunities if you decide for yourself whether a job fits your present needs and not open yourself to conflict by discussing decisions you are in the middle of—except of course with the people your decisions affect directly. Strengthen your mind by reminding yourself that you are in the best position to know what you should be doing. And after you have started a job, save yourself the pangs of doubt by talking as little as possible about the inevitable problems that accompany a transition of this sort. Few people can resist an opportunity to sow confusion. So do not give them one. Do not be afraid to stay close to your heart and to keep your own counsel.

Do not be afraid to know. Do not be afraid to doubt. And do not be afraid to turn to the stillness within you and ask for help.

The Problem with Getting the Right Job

Another hindrance to finding a job, although perhaps a less conscious one, is the premise that the job choice one is making is permanent. Out there awaits some lasting and just-right niche. The only real problem is locating it. And yet, there really is no right job.

"This is right" implies "This is permanent." It shouldn't, but it does. How many of us could believe that we had finally found the right job or, worse, were "guided" or "led" to it and still feel free to quit at the end of the first day? Given this approach, it should not be surprising that most people's major concern is to avoid making a mistake. If you believe in the existence of a right job, you will also look on other jobs as "wrong," at least for you.

Look at the position this attitude puts us in. Since there is a job that is best for us, most of the work that comes to our attention is a potential mistake and our life is like walking through a minefield. Should we already have a job, we can't help harboring the suspicion that we chose wrongly. We think we can somehow believe in the existence of a right course of action in one area of our life yet not believe in it in every other area.

Because this is impossible, most people suspect they also married the wrong person (which means they must have the wrong children), bought or rented the wrong place to live in (so the neighbors aren't what they should be), and probably ate the wrong cereal for breakfast. I don't think any of us has managed to escape this outlook entirely.

No more absolute and awful tyranny reigns than our fear of being wrong. We have a simple choice. We can try to avoid all mistakes or we can relax. In seeking a job it is good to drop the notion that the universe has tucked away some haloed position just for you. Now at least you will not be haunted by the vague feeling that somehow you are not going about this job-finding business in the correct way. There are a thousand correct ways because there are a thousand peaceful ways.

Do not remain in fear. The elimination of fear is the beginning of vision, and to give ourselves a broad range of options permits us to see opportunities we were blind to before. It is not uncommon for an individual who is unable to find a paying job to take volunteer work or to begin helping someone for free and suddenly have a salaried position. Or sometimes several at once become available, much like the classic example of the couple who cannot bear children, decide to adopt, and instantly become fertile. Once again, there is not a spiritual law at work in these instances, but to the degree our mind is relieved of fear, we feel and experience more connection and more harmony. And it is an observable fact that action often—although not always—lifts fear. (For example, adopting might *increase* some couples' fear.)

The willingness to act in a simple, direct way usually loosens the mind's grip on its problems. The precise external results are not predictable—an adoption does not automatically render a couple fertile, and volunteer work does not consistently manifest a paying job. Nevertheless, openness to starting and continuing the small steps involved in walking around a problem will eventually result in leaving the problem behind. Overt manifestations of willingness reduce inner conflict, and an unconflicted mind can step over any hindrance.

DECISIONS

How to Make a Decision

We humans have a very interesting and peculiar way of deciding what to do in life. Decisions come far more rapidly than most people realize at first. They are in fact continuous. Thus our individual choices are not as important as they seem. Yet our *approach* to making all decisions is vital, for it lays before us the terrain we must travel.

This isn't to say that some decisions are not more life affecting than others, for in terms of how they influence the outward course of things, they are indeed. They are not, however, more happiness affecting.

It isn't necessary to have one way of deciding what color potatoes to buy and another way for choosing a job. Actually, the belief that a more perfect answer is required for a larger question initiates the turmoil we get ourselves into. Regardless of how dramatic the circumstances surrounding a question, all we need is an answer that *comes from peace*. Perhaps the one difference in how choices about work, divorce, operations, money, moving, and other anxiety-riddled subjects should be made is that more care should be taken to see that they are done in the *same* peaceful way. When deciding fearful questions, the temptation is greater to fall back into the old habit of deciding them fearfully.

Our usual approach to choosing what to do is to consider alternatives. This reaction is so imbedded in us that it's difficult even to raise doubt as to its practicality. If it were no more than a calm reviewing of options, it would cause no harm. But it is not calm, and it quickly *eliminates* good options. Awareness, concentration, and sustained effort are needed to break this habit.

Notice that after just a few moments of considering alternatives, the mind becomes scattered and inefficient. The reason for this is that there is no end of things to consider. We sense that we have taken our seat on a never-ending merry-go-round. The potential for scaring ourselves is great, since we are anxious to escape this mental snare. Thus we frequently make a second mistake. We act in the face of our conflict. Because it has that look about it, we call this "being decisive."

But a decision made in conflict produces conflicted results, thereby adding to our mental chaos, whereas a decision arrived at in a gentle and restful state of mind doesn't disrupt our core of happiness. Once you develop the habit of deciding all things with your quietness, your life—including relationships, health, and finances—will begin to smooth out and simplify. You will not magically be given advantages over other people, but the outward circumstances of your life, which your decisions affect, will increasingly accommodate rather than sabotage your desire to be happy.

To make good decisions we must train ourselves to focus on our state of mind rather than on the unanswered question. As long as our attention is on the question, our mind remains unfit to choose in the interest of happiness. This is not "harmless," because our experience is a continuous outpouring of our mental environment.

Deciding from peace eventually becomes automatic, but much practice is needed. It is less fear provoking to practice first with smaller everyday choices before applying this new procedure to major life-affecting ones such as choosing a job.

Decision Guidelines

To this end, here is a summary of decision-making guidelines. Most of them have been touched on previously, but not in one place.

- When you see that you have a question, stop. Do this *before* you begin considering alternatives and their ramifications, because shortly after you start worrying, your mind becomes fear dominated and it's more difficult to go back and make an unconflicted decision.

- Settle and still your mind. Use any mental or physical trick that helps. You don't have to attain some mystical state of calm, but you do have to take enough time to be sure that you are as peaceful as you are able to be at this moment.

- Look very closely at the problem. Take your time and make sure that you see all parts of it clearly. Remember not to scare yourself by imagining consequences that could result from various solutions. In fact, don't think about answers at all. Just examine the problem calmly and thoroughly. If you need to do a little formal research, do so happily.

- Look into your heart and ask yourself if there is anything you want to do about this problem now, today. Trying to decide before it's time to decide will do no more than pollute the present.

- If there is nothing you wish to do, or if it's not yet clear what you want to do, decide to wait. Never be afraid to wait. But remember that waiting is a decision, so be sure to do it without conflict. It's okay to decide quickly, and it's okay to wait. Peace is the only consideration.

- If you do want to act in the present, be certain that you are not limiting your options in any way. It may help to list as many of these as possible, but do not rank or evaluate them.

- If you see that there is something specific you want to try first, carry it out easily and happily.

- Do not reconsider. Instead of attempting to judge whether your decision was correct, recall that your mental state was sound when you made it and questionable now that you are worrying.

- If what you try doesn't sufficiently lessen the problem, simply try something else.

If you keep doing this—deciding from your peace what you wish to do in the present and acting on it with assurance—you will eventually put the problem behind you. This is as inevitable as light dispelling darkness.

Deciding Where to Be

If you are seeking a job, don't make the mistake of presuming there is a way to *recognize* the position that awaits you. Attempting to do this is attempting to rely on magic through a kind of divining of signs.

By miraculous coincidence the regular receptionist is absent, and in talking to the substitute I discover that this person's mother has the same unusual first name as my mother. "Ah," I think, "this is the job I'm meant to have." And during the interview I blow my chances by saying so. Or knowing that my reasoning was not perfect or the "signs" not complete, if I do get the position, I remain fearful that this may not be the one the angels were indicating. And this uncertainty hinders my performance and gets me fired.

You will be taking no risk, and you will definitely increase your happiness, if you assume that wherever you are today you are supposed to be and whatever work you are doing is "right." Then do the job at hand honestly. No gain comes from dampening down our spirit or from feeding our minds reasons to doubt. Doing something well never blocks, but only increases, our ability to discern that the time has now come to move on, should that time come.

So often we believe that in order to turn from something we must first find fault with it. If we quit we must denounce our former employer; a friend must become a disappointment before we can stop being romantically involved; a spiritual organization or teacher must be presumed dangerous if we feel like moving on. But why should our participation make something good and our leaving make it bad? A happy person enters and leaves in peace.

None of this implies that there are no genuine indicators as to whether you should give a particular job a try or leave the one you are in. A sense of comfort about the people with whom you would be working is often a reliable form of inner knowing. But it will not tell you how far you will advance, how long you will be employed there, or even whether you will be hired in the first place.

This sense is not mystical but rather the beginning of true intelligence. It is a feeling something like this: You see that your mind comes to rest when you think of this place and these people. It is *not* a feeling of excitement about your prospective good fortune. Nor is it even a "liking" of the people or the facilities. You merely find that you are *comfortable* with the thought of taking this job. It is an adequate job for now.

This calm instinct about people and places can of course be applied to other circumstances besides employment. To do so does not provide objective knowledge about the world, because an uncomfortable situation for one person is not so regarded by another. Nor does this sense of things entail analyzing and discussing personalities. And it most definitely is not the sad cataloging of individuals for what some refer to as their "enemies list."

I am speaking of the ability to see things as they are in the present and not the tiring habit of avoiding certain people or establishments because of something disagreeable that once happened. It is simply a natural realization of whether a particular relationship, a certain place, a specific kind of situation will make it easier or more difficult for us to be happy.

Such understanding is not fodder for gossip, nor are diehard rules of behavior formulated as a result. This same calm knowing is sensitive to the changes continually occurring in individuals and places. Once it's developed, it is a valuable sensitivity that can gently guide you to where you wish to do your banking, buy your groceries and your gas, what restaurants you want to frequent, as well as what job you wish to take or continue. If where we place ourselves over and over is disturbing, it's unlikely that the overall happiness of our life will remain unaffected.

As you go about running your usual errands for the next week or two, mentally (and whenever feasible, physically) pause once you are within each place—store, laundry, gas station, friend's house, church, bank—and gently ask yourself, "Is this a happy place?" Do not give yourself a verbal answer, but carry the question into the place the way you might wear a new pair of glasses.

Be conscious of any tendency to form the answer from your memory of what has taken place there in the past, or from whether your eyes like the "class" of people and décor, or what the cost in time or money is to you, or a hundred other factors irrelevant to the overall atmosphere into which you have just walked. You wish merely to be sensitive to the degree of ease or discontent, peace or anger, good or ill will—in other words, to the degree of happiness that surrounds you.

Immediately after you leave, stop again and ask, "Have I just left a happy place?" Do not answer the question in your mind, but let it come to you quietly in its own time. Once you believe you have seen the answer, if you find yourself talking against this place to others, I can assure you that you have seen nothing as yet, because the kind of vision I am speaking of is not a judgment. Nor is it a decision about what is wrong or right for other people. It is only a simple recognition of what is best for you at this time.

If you realize that a place is not happy, this of course does not always mean that it would be easier on you to not frequent it. For example, it will not make you more content with life to abruptly stop visiting your parent or child even though you might see that this relative's home is unhappy and that it's difficult for you to be there. Nor does recognizing the pervading mood of a place imply that you now have reason to fear it. By becoming more aware of the atmosphere you have chosen to enter, perhaps you will now take the time to clear your mind of all conflict so that as you walk into this place you bring your ease and enjoyment with you and, as you leave, you carry no emotion that could chip away at your happiness.

No Decision Is an Island

Work hours, times of worship, the time one comes home to one's partner, dinner hours, and the like are ordinarily thought of as separate islands of purpose or choice within the day. But this idea makes any unifying theme to one's life an impossibility. Thus it would appear feasible to limit oneself to just a few key purposes at key times. It might seem enough to have a nutritious meal in the morning, to pursue one's career during the day, in the evening to be entertained, and then to get a good night's sleep. But as an approach to life, to want even a limited amount of fragmentation gives us a mindset that contains no safeguards, no self-limiting boundaries.

If you are like most of us, a typical segment of the day is likely to go like this: You come home from work and see that you are out of toilet paper. It's an hour before the evening news and you calculate that you can just make it to Safeway and back. You pick up the keys and walk to the car. Now, as you get in and turn on the ignition, what is foremost in your mind, what is your purpose in life? Is it to idle the car long enough to eliminate the risk of wear to the engine? Or is it to put the car in gear immediately to cut back on the risk of being late for the news?

Your inner conflict is almost unconscious, even though there is a slight but perceptible undercurrent of guilt as you choose saving time over prolonging the life of the engine and bolt from the driveway. Or a little stab of anxiety as you just sit there idling the car while the seconds tick away and the first and most important segment of the news begins flowing away from you like an ice cream cone held uneaten in the sun.

If your spouse is with you, and if his or her ego position on this differs, a thought critical of you such as "How did I marry someone so cheap?" or "You've never liked this car because I'm the one who picked it out" flicks through your spouse's mind practically unnoticed but not entirely unfelt by you.

At the first intersection you wonder which way you should turn. Is your purpose in life now to protect your self-image? For if it is, you should not turn right and go to Ralph's Food Market, even though it's 10 minutes closer, because the last time you were there you told Ralph you were never coming back. This time the "wrong" decision might even draw a comment from your spouse.

As you drive to Safeway, should physical safety take precedence over making the lights? Perhaps a brief argument breaks out in the car over this one. "You ran a red light again, Dear." "No, Dear, I didn't. It was yellow as I entered the intersection." A long silence, then quite innocently you ask, "Were you able to get an appointment with Dr., uh, what's-her-name, you know, Dear, your ophthalmologist friend?" Because suddenly the purpose of life is to be right.

At last you are in the Safeway lot and now your life purpose is to get the parking place nearest the entrance. But as you turn to back into it someone pulls in ahead of you, even though you clearly had the right of way. You are so angry about this that—for the moment—this grievance is more important than the latest war that was just announced on your car radio.

The point we are forever missing is that the whole of life is always "for the moment." While we stay lost in what is already over and done with ("They moved the toilet paper. Why is this store always reorganizing its stock?") or in what is yet to be ("The news is in 12 minutes and as usual there's no checkout person at the express lane.") our life remains patiently in the moment waiting for us to recognize it.

The unhappiness of this entire situation was caused not by Ralph or the lights or the speedy parker. It was caused by the same mental state that continues to torture us as we wheel into our driveway, just missing the neighbor's wiener dog, only to find that the news has been preempted by a funeral special.

We are upset, yet we have so many purposes that we don't even know if we want to watch the news. We have never paused long enough to look into our heart to see. A true purpose is a decision made with grandeur instead of smallness.

Hopeless Mistakes

There are no permanent mistakes. If something begins as a mistaken decision, and perhaps everything we do does to some degree, it doesn't have to remain that way. Yet the moment a mistake transforms into a spurt of learning is up to us.

It's important to keep in mind that *changing* the original form of what we suspect was a mistake (by quitting our job, dumping our partner, moving, trading in our car) is not an essential first step. We are not learning what is a good or bad outward form for things to take. We are in fact already weighed down with these kinds of fragmented lessons. The advance in learning that takes us to another level of happiness is the transfer of mental wholeness, already recognizable under some circumstances, into new areas of our life.

Naturally this doesn't mean there are no changes that would make things easier. However, our level of happiness remains unaffected if all we do is make changes. Most people's first response to a feeling of discontent is to start rummaging around in their lives for what's wrong. Since nothing there is perfect, they quickly find fault with something and trying to change it becomes their primary focus. Some form of this syndrome constitutes the bulk of activity in most people's lives—either hurrying around to fix the latest perceived affliction or turning away in resignation because it's probably hopeless.

Happiness becomes much simpler once we realize that it

starts with a strong, whole, peaceful state of mind and then, very gently, extends outward. If a change is undertaken it's because it may make our way a little simpler, and not "to set things right." If we begin in a worried, agitated state, the changes we make carry with them an air of anxiety and defeat. All we see is that they, too, are not perfect, and once again we begin a disjointed search for what more can be rectified. Or we turn away and suffer a little death.

"Make your living with your left foot" is an ancient Eastern saying. Don't let your livelihood be the aim of your existence. Do your job well, in fact, do it magnificently, but don't take it out of context and make it the end you seek. The same can be said for our health, car, wardrobe, or reputation. If we wish to be happy, our function must remain the same under all circumstances.

We carry with us an atmosphere—one that is strong and whole or one that is fragmented. Since this is our choice, we must be conscious of which we carry. Let not circumstances choose for us, or we will feel scattered and to some degree unreal. Often the reason we seem of no contribution is that we contribute very little from our heart. Yet *events* seem to snatch away the best of us before we can extend it.

Please allow me to repeat one suggestion. Decide on one all-encompassing motive for all that you do. Do this today, and your way will instantly become simpler. Why are you here? Do you know what your purpose is? What would you like it to be? Because that is what it will be. Live, work, and breathe for your life, for your loved ones, for the strangers you encounter, for all of you. Most people have never stopped to ask why they bother to go on doing *anything*. Consequently nothing they do is ever for the same purpose twice. Make the present happy by making it the same as every other part of your life.

CHAPTER

12

MONEY

What Is Money For?

The world sends out two basic messages about money. First: Nothing is more desirable. And second: Isn't that a shame; it really shouldn't be that way. So always we want more of it, but always it remains tainted.

Of all the topics on which the mind can dwell, money is one of the most miserable. "I could use some more money" produces a dull distress in almost every heart. Few have remained untouched by all the contradictions and guilt that swirl around the subject. Most of us can't even go out and purchase a few vegetables without feeling a tinge of self-disgust for not having driven the extra miles necessary to buy them for less. Or if we did go out of our way to get "a better value," we have fleeting thoughts of how tight we are or how uncharitably we use our time. After all, Mother Teresa never wasted a day trying to find carrots at 3 cents less a pound.

I remember well an early realization of just how unhappy a

preoccupation with money can be. It was pointed out to me when I was still quite young that I had three wealthy relatives. Questions of who would inherit, and how much, were often discussed with overtones of great excitement within our family. And so my daydreams began.

Even a very young person can recognize that these thoughts offer no refuge. To fantasize about this kind of thing, you must wish for someone to die and for others to be out of favor. Then of course there are the guilty considerations of whether you *deserve* to have a lot of money come to you in this way, which, as it turned out, was a worry I need never have bothered myself about.

Possibly you have seen firsthand how insensitively people can act when property is being divided: picking and squabbling over the deceased's furniture and jewelry and in the process forming grudges and personal shames that can be carried for a lifetime. But this is just one of the numerous pathetic outcomes of our culture's inordinate fascination with money. There are also the tactics many are tempted to use to get a promotion, the unkind way we parade our purchases before friends, and the years we absent ourselves from loved ones in pursuit of . . . what?

This is the central question that goes unasked about money: What is it for? We believe that we never have enough, that somehow we must get more, and that we will rest easy only when we have more than enough. But how much is "more than enough"? And does that concept even have meaning? The fact is that our desired destination is so vague that there is no way we can ever reach it.

My sister-in-law told me that a friend of hers called one day and asked if she would like to go with him to meet "a really wealthy man." On their way over she could see that her friend was very excited. "This man makes over twelve million a year!"

he said. Clearly he was unimpressed with the two-and-a-half million a year he himself made.

The point is not that money is somehow bad but that the desire for money contains within it no stopping place. Yet nearly everyone has need of at least some money. And so the failure to ask "What is it for?" can lead to still another unhappy predisposition: the belief that money defiles, that it is at best a necessary evil, and that to give up as many symbols of prosperity as possible somehow makes one a better person.

Specifically, this point of view may include notions that it's a "higher path" not to consider salary when selecting a job. That to resist putting money in tax shelters, investments, or even savings is less self-seeking, less spiritually stultifying. That having a large wardrobe, owning a luxury car, or living in an affluent neighborhood are reliable signs of personal shallowness. This outlook is sometimes pushed to the point where all purchases are made with inordinate concern and only out of the strictest necessity. Anything brand new, such as a new car or TV, is automatically viewed with suspicion. It can even be applied to the amount of food one eats or the number of hours one sleeps— less of both indicating a more spiritually minded individual.

To ask "What is it for?" puts money back into context. Money is simply a means, a medium, a way. If we stop to worship the road that leads to a desired location, we never arrive. Likewise, our progress ceases if we pause to detest it. Many people make a similar mistake in expecting something from particular days of the week or times of the year. The holiday season, Saturday night, their birthday, the equinox, or some other number on a calendar is given importance in itself, and subconsciously they bide their time awaiting some undefined acknowledgment from the universe. But on this day, as on every other day, the Earth revolves and the sun sets without incident.

The highest number of suicides occurs around Christmas. I

know from my work on a crisis hot line that many people who feel suicidal that time of year have had, once again, a great expectation dashed. Although they are unable to see this, it had to be dashed. The 25th of December is incapable of doing anything. And so, too, is the number on a bill or stock certificate. It is bloodless, lifeless, and totally innocent. It's just a number.

Unlike people, money is what money does. These little metal disks and slips of paper are merely a way of obtaining certain externals, but not the only way. Their helpfulness or hurtfulness cannot exceed the tiny range of things they can bring to us. There have been countless songs and jokes, as well as essays, sermons, and books on what money can't buy. And this is indeed helpful to recognize. So much of the disappointment brought by the pursuit of or flight from money comes from associating it with irrelevancies such as self-respect, future happiness, finding a person who truly loves us, being a winner, or in some other way feeling more satisfied than others.

Fear of Money

There are so many wealthy people who are obviously unhappy that this recognition can lead to the assumption that if we find ways of renouncing money we decrease our chances of being miserable. It is true that, just like anything else that sets us apart, having enormous wealth makes life more difficult. Yet how could merely reducing our financial options bring to us something of value? The ancient wisdom that love of money is behind much of the evil of the world is true. And so, too, are hate and fear of money. Can quitting one's job and turning instead to grubbing, scrounging, and groveling bring peace of mind? Those who do usually become so obsessed with obtaining simple necessities that their minds drown in the world rather than rise above it. Seeking more than enough or less than enough cannot set the issue of money to rest. Only the lessening of fear around the entire subject will help.

A good overall rule might be, *Money is not important; therefore, do whatever allows you not to be preoccupied with it.* Many problems in life can be resolved by our accepting a daily solution rather than continuing to chase after a permanent one. For example, there may be a permanent answer to dental hygiene, but most people would rather brush their teeth every day than to search for some final resolution. They are not in conflict about this, so the time spent in front of the bathroom sink is not a burden. Many people who know in their hearts that they are alcoholics hold themselves in misery by insisting that there must be a way for them to continue drinking. Possibly there is, but those who decide that from now on they will attend an AA meeting every night settle the question and go on with their lives.

Likewise, a job, even though it can consume half one's waking life, is an excellent way of diminishing anxiety about where the necessary funds will come from. Most of the alternatives people turn to such as get-rich-quick schemes, marrying for money, gambling in various forms, and skirting the law are far more fear provoking than simply going to work every day. Of course it's possible to obtain all the money one will ever need virtually overnight. But short of inheriting it or winning the lottery, this is so contrary to the general course of things that people usually spend as much time trying to get rich quickly, and not succeeding, as they would at a regular job, and more time by far worrying.

In recent years the yearning for a way of life that is good and positively affecting has grown enormously. Many now find themselves wanting not only to be of help but also to be of help in a direct and consistent way. Along with this desire, which in most cases is sincere and deeply felt, there can be considerable ego involvement. At the same time, there is a widespread belief that runs like this: "If you will just relax and trust a little, somehow it will all work out. And if perchance it doesn't, you will see that this, too, was a good thing."

That bit of wisdom is actually true, but it is not true on the level of experience to which it is usually applied. What is implied here is that there are ways, especially mental or spiritual ways, to have all our worldly desires met without following the usual worldly procedures. In fact, it is often part of this belief that the requisite inner state may be jeopardized if you do go by the rules.

Consequently, we now see many people living without economy, keeping inadequate or no track at all of their income and expenses, possessing no clear idea of where their money is going, or giving up their jobs altogether and waiting anxiously for God or the universe to care for them. And there may even be a period in which all of this appears to work wonderfully well. Discounted, however, are the times they must scurry about for money or, in some cases, sustain an almost nonstop fear about the future.

We can't hope to stabilize our life if there is an inherent pattern of fear already set up. The truth is that a daily sense of economy is more conducive to peace than a daily sense of waste. We can't add to our happiness by destroying what we think of as real.

In order to reach the degree of happiness that tranquillity can bring, the question of how our needs are to be met should not be approached in a wishful manner. To conduct our affairs so that we feel secure about our income, and so that our spending practices seem wise and good, cannot possibly hinder our capacity to develop a higher trust or to flow easily with life's circumstances. A stable source of income is less apt to spawn mental conflict than an unstable one. These ideas are not a call for sacrifice and scrimping, nor does anyone need to become mercenary. Rather, they are a plea for simplicity and intelligence.

There is no magic to money. The problem of earning and keeping money can be resolved without resort to mental trickery and an interminable study of occult rules. The Divine does not have to be entreated or manipulated in order for us to be at ease in our financial dealings. But it must also become clear that we can't separate ourselves from our money problems. Financial chaos activates the fearful part of us and thereby constricts genuine happiness.

The Chronic Pattern

As we discussed earlier, the world's two controlling attitudes about money are that it's wonderful and it's evil. Although these are contradictory, they are only different sides of the same misplaced emphasis, and very few people escape being infected by both views. The usual way we act them out is that we strive to get more and more but feel guilty about what we have obtained and unconsciously attempt to rid ourselves of it. Until a fundamental shift in emphasis occurs, this pattern usually remains unchanged regardless of the amount of money that comes our way.

With the people you know well perhaps you have noticed that certain individuals tend always to be on time or always late, and you can often predict their arrival within a few minutes. For example, those friends who usually come 20 minutes late will remain fairly consistent even though their excuses each time may vary widely. The circumstances they cite are manifestly not the governing factor. The value they place on time determines how they use it, and their pattern will not change until the value itself changes. For example, as they start to recognize that time can be a means of kindness, their arrival time becomes more caring.

This is equally true of spending habits. A young couple starting out will quickly form a pattern of retaining a certain percentage of what comes in or of being a certain percentage in
debt. This ratio will not vary by much even though their earn-
ings may increase substantially over the years. If suddenly they
receive a financial windfall, their financial "system" will begin
digesting it. As soon as this is completed—and a windfall can
be finished off in a remarkably short period—they go back to
the same pattern of indebtedness (or percentage of surplus) that
existed before.

Although the form it takes can change at any time, the desire
for externals remains the same until desire itself is questioned.
This is true whether the wanting is for ever more money or for
ridding oneself of money. Almost always it is for both, and the
degree to which these two wishes cancel each other out determines whether the individual is always a little short, a little
ahead, has needless surfeit, or just breaks even, none of which
is either good or bad. The problem is not in the outcome that
these conflicting attitudes produce but in the valuing of money,
either positively or negatively, for its own sake.

Take anything out of context and trouble begins. If we have
a recurring money problem, we can be sure we have singled
money out in some way. Just seeing that much can be of help
because we are not so quick to blame a certain person or special
set of circumstances for why the problem has occurred this time.

Ending Financial Soap Operas

When starting a self-improvement process, many people make
the mistake of siding with the angry voice within them in an
attempt to bring about behavioral changes. Most of us still
believe we can denounce ourselves into being more responsible. But self-loathing, even mild self-loathing, does not truly

motivate. And it usually backfires. It can have a temporary effect at best because it comes from the side of our nature that values conflict and attack. From conflict arises pain, and pain can take us only so far. Lasting change must be grounded in happiness. A new course must reward and continue to satisfy or it will be turned away from.

The following series of suggestions is designed to increase awareness—always the first step in healing—and to arrive at a plan that stops the destructive behavior. This procedure is not intended to plumb deep psychological causes, but to open the mind to practical possibilities.

- First, you want to increase your awareness of your attitude toward money in general. As you go through the day, begin looking at exactly what is happening around you and within you whenever you are the least bit excited or fearful about finances. Look more closely, be more present, as you make a purchase, pay a bill, watch a financial report on TV, balance your checkbook, drive past a bank. Examples:

  "No matter what mail I have received, I always open the bills first."

  "The service seems worse and I leave a skimpy tip when I'm worried about anything, whether money related or not."

  "I feel dislike and resentment toward older white people who drive new, upper-end cars."

- After you have done this for a few days, close your eyes and think in a general way about these experiences, as well as any past experiences concerning money that come to mind. Simply allow various scenes to cross your awareness, whether of recent observations or of old events.

- As you do this, be conscious of your anxiety level and pay special attention to the images that are the most broadly disturbing. You are not looking for just one or two embarrassing or difficult moments but for a pattern, a recurring unhappiness in your life. For example,

  Needing to offer things of monetary value in an attempt to cement relationships;

  Being periodically short and having to forage about for money;

  Always scrimping in an insensitive, unkind way;

  A history of spending sprees, especially when you are unhappy;

  Recurring feelings of superiority or inferiority based on money.

- Taking up one of the patterns you notice, perhaps the one that is the most pervasive and time consuming, ask yourself in what context it occurs. In other words, what are the kinds of thoughts and feelings, and what are the circumstances, that precede and surround an outbreak of this pattern? For instance,

  "When I am physically tired and discouraged."

  "After I have fantasized about how a truly advanced person would live."

  "While I'm shopping for clothes in a mall."

  "When I'm in public and think I am being judged."

- Your goal here is not to engage in deep analysis but merely to look for obvious triggers of this one pattern. You may notice that you usually go on a spending spree just after a bad argument with your partner. Or you notice that you overreact to getting a lot of money at once, for instance at payday. As you think about each instance of the pattern, pay attention to anything you can remember feeling just prior to, or during, the times you have acted out this problem. And remember to do all of this without self-censure. You are just looking. You are only gathering information.

- Using whatever relaxation technique or mental trick you wish, quiet your body and mind and rest for a few seconds.

- Now ask yourself if there are some simple ways to bypass the circumstances that trigger the problem. You are not necessarily interested in discovering how to change the circumstances themselves so much as in seeing how to avoid them. For example, if you frequently overspend when you have to walk through the mall but tend not to overspend when you drive to an isolated store, one way to avoid the trigger is obvious—shop at stores that are not in malls. This is not a rule you want to make for yourself. It's just a thought about a possibility.

- Describe to yourself a few other ways that you could avoid or nullify the circumstances that appear to generate your problem. In trying to think of these, it may help open your mind to start with ridiculous and fanciful options, then try to add a few that are more reasonable.

    "I could pretend to be blind, use a white cane, and have people direct me to the store. Only upon entering the store could I open my eyes."

    "As I walk toward the store I want, I could pretend that if I stare at any display window of any shop for more than three seconds, I will instantly turn to stone."

"As I walk, I could study the floor surfaces of the mall—materials used, scuff marks, colors, surface coatings, and so forth."

"I could buy everything online."

"I could make a few phone calls and compose a list of all the places that are likely to have what I want that are not in malls."

"I could use a combination of two or three of these options."

- Sitting quietly, taking all the time you need, ask yourself what do you now want to do about this problem. Remember to allow yourself any option, then decide on one simple step—not an infallible step, not a step you hope will solve everything forever, but merely one you think has a chance of bringing improvement. Let's say your recurring problem is that you run short of money, and let's say your income is seasonal rather than monthly. A beginning step might be to open a second bank account into which you place all income and out of which you pay yourself a fixed monthly salary. Let it be a plan that you are confident is within your present readiness to carry out. Write out this plan, maybe as a contract with yourself. Sign it. Then try it.

- Keep trying new measures until you are past the behavior. Perhaps write down the dates and steps you take and the results you get with each measure. Finally, record the date when you believe the problem is behind you. You need not be absolutely certain of this, but do wait until you have a sense of honesty about making this last entry.

Money is a problem in perception. The ultimate solution to most financial difficulties is to view them with enough honesty that our mind can focus calmly and see what to do. Fear is constricted awareness. Honesty is the willingness to broaden awareness. Naturally there are situations that would terrify anyone, and the specter of being financially destitute is one of them. But short of life-threatening and identity-threatening money problems, most of the financially disturbed areas of our life can be brought to peace. Once fear is eliminated, or sufficiently lessened, there are few problems that can't be solved. That is quite different from saying, "There isn't anything you can't get to go the way your ego wants it to go." By "solved" I mean "made happy." Options are always present to make any area of our life happier, and they are seen as we practice being honest with ourselves.

CHAPTER 13

POSSESSIONS

Inner Simplicity

What's the point of money if there are no signs of it in your life? "If you've got it, flaunt it."

So reasons the world. No good for money to lie there like some overfed cat. To get our money's worth from money there has to be hard visual evidence that it's a power we personally wield. Perhaps a portfolio page on our PC with Internet-driven spread sheets, flow charts, and market streaming. Or at least a consoling bank balance printed in a little gilded book. Something, anything, we can look at in private moments, that makes us feel warm and fuzzy, like pictures of gardens and grandchildren.

But if not that, then surely an occasional highly conversable vacation including "marvelous" food. Or the latest PDA, SUV, Webcam, or data watch. Good seats and good service. Respect for one's business opinion. Even an ornate spouse will do. Otherwise we feel cheated.

Money seems to call out to us to be translated into some thing. We think it's a tragedy for money to just remain money. Or if money has become important to us as a symbol of what to avoid, this attitude must also have its display. Perhaps bare-bones and rigidly secondhand furnishings. The kind of clothes that indicate one is not interested in clothes. Only backyard-grown or bulk-bought foods. Clearly no hair spray. Or a meticulous avoidance of designer-name boutiques and little French restaurants. From this point of view, money should be translated into a sacrifice of options. Here again, it's unacceptable for money to be just money.

The desire for more and more (or its corollary, the desire to be deprived) has as its root a belief that "what you see is what you get." Yet form is not everything. Form is valuable only to the degree that it serves the interests of content. Content is everything, and inner simplicity is the permanent sigh of relief that this has been recognized.

People who have reached an advanced stage of happiness invariably lead simple lives. Their household environment and personal affairs are free of chaos and clutter. They eat simply, dress peacefully, and follow a harmonious routine. If compassion requires that they break with any of this, they can do so easily and quickly, because for the truly happy person simplicity is not just another fetish, it is an enduring internal state.

Whenever we are afraid, we are to some degree tense and intractable. That is why a scattered approach to life is rigid, whereas a simple one is not. Yet this is not recognized by many people. They think that accumulating is satisfying, that buying an endless list of things they don't want and can't use spells real freedom. Or they make the equal mistake of drawing back in fear from all signs of wealth.

Another word for simplicity is clarity. Deep inner clarity about one's purpose and way. Now there is space to see.

Simplicity is freedom from mental and emotional litter. The heart has room to love and enjoy. Simplicity is also guileless and straightforward. It is the uncomplicated way, the easy step, and this soft internal order is expressed outwardly in an instinctive avoidance of excess or its counterpart, deprivation and self-imposed loss. However, because simplicity is a core condition, there can be no formula for how it takes form within one's lifestyle.

Simplicity of heart has a calming effect on one's environment, but the particulars will vary with each individual. There are no rules for determining how many changes of clothes must hang in the closet, whether one should own a yogurt maker, or if mounting Uncle Toby's stuffed moose head in the den is immoral.

Yet it's there to be seen by anyone who cares to look that all possessions are subject to loss and deterioration. Hair and toothbrush bristles develop split ends, cars fall apart, guppies die, running shoes wear out, and the neighbors you acquire along with your new house pressure you either to keep your grass edged or to tear out the lawn altogether and put in crushed red lava stone.

Even though it would seem too obvious to miss, these flapping, distracting streamers tied to every new possession are almost never considered as we go about the supposedly happy work of accumulating ever more. And still we wonder why we can't go through a single day in peace.

From time to time purchases must be made. That's obvious. But this does not negate the fact that consequences attend. We can't even bring home a few cut flowers without ramifications. In what will they be placed? Must some chemical be added to the water? In whose room will they go? Should the cat be allowed to nibble? Which family member's role is it to remove the wilted ones?

However, it never seems to be this intrinsic nature of possessions that gets our attention. Only the latest symptom of it is noticed. So when the refrigerator suddenly starts making a strange noise, we think that all it takes for life again to be worth living is to get someone out to fix it. And of course, it should be taken care of.

Yet what do we do? At the recommendation of the repairman who demonstrated his reliability by keeping the appointment only after the fourth call and a few threats, we purchase a new refrigerator, the three-door Maxi Deluxe 500-X with Chooz-a-shape icemaker and chilled-water busboy. Far more can now go wrong than could before. But it stands so shiny and handsome in the corner of our kitchen that we don't think of this until several weeks later when the "busboy" refuses to drop crushed ice in our Dixie cup and the repairman we called before now tells us he isn't certified to work on the 500-X.

Is Our Home Our Haven?

We are often so tyrannized by our home that we can't be comfortable within it. We walk into a room and see only a collection of mistakes. Or we have a nagging little question about the chairs. The décor is atrophying and we're not sure what to do. Our mind is filled with equal parts fear and decorating hints. In a very real sense we do not have a home because we are uncertain what this place we live in is for. A showcase of our talent and creativity? An example of our energy consciousness? A display case for our wealth? Or merely a place to sleep?

We truly want to feel welcomed by our own home. We want it to be a place of relaxation and rest. We want to be able to "come home." But as long as we view it through the eyes of anxiety or condemnation, we will not be able to.

One of many unhappy solutions to this dynamic is to begin

neglecting the things we do own because we suddenly decide "I no longer care about worldly things. I'm beyond all of that." It's true that in this way less of our day is devoted to maintenance and repair, but the underlying distress we feel when we withhold our love from our very surroundings delays us more than remaining aware of what is occurring within our habitat and caring for the things that need care.

An equally unhappy solution is to begin fearing or, worse, hating possessions and refusing to acquire what would be a comfort and help to ourselves and those around us. Once again, there is no list of what these things might be because this will vary with each family or individual. For a long time I resisted buying a computer. Once I acquired one I began turning out my columns and manuscripts in about half the time it took before. I owe this to Gayle, who got me to look closely at my reasons for not wanting one. There was a self-image—that of the log-cabin and candlelight kind of guy—that I did not want shattered. When I saw this honestly, I recognized how silly it was and bought the equipment that would help me do my job.

Yet a sense of home is neither a new computer nor a gadget-free environment. Home is an openness of heart that easily discerns what will add to the ease around us or what will merely complicate our way.

A genuine feel for home or embracing simplicity is fairly easy to develop provided we take it in small steps. This being a chapter on possessions, let's begin with these. Naturally, any other area of your life—your relationships, diet, finances, health—could just as easily become the starting point.

What Have We Put Around Us?

While it's true that we are affected by our possessions on an unconscious level, it is not true that we must remain forever unaware of what these influences are and where they come from. Because we tolerate them, they come from us. The dreams we have at night are a good example of one way we set up an environment for ourselves, then choose to forget our part in forming it. In our dreams the surrounding events and atmospheres appear to be happening to us. This is harmless in the case of dreams (except perhaps in certain extreme forms), but certainly it is not without effects within our daily life.

It is possible to have positive associations with what some people would consider messy surroundings. Clutter to one is austerity to another. What is important to our happiness is not these comparisons but our personal sense of an environment that is in harmony with our mind. When we are learning happiness, our mind is in a vulnerable state. We are more affected by the things around us and how closely they match our sense of order and cleanliness than we may realize at first. So until we learn to see, it's perhaps best to look at fewer things.

Few people suffer from progressive austerity. The common ailment is over-accumulation. It is therefore important to consider the number of things around you and also the comfortableness of the memories you have about each item. Both are equally affecting. If you have an overall sense of excess or the perception that there are spots where things are too crowded, and if you believe these conditions exist in part because you have been negligent, it's unlikely that you won't occasionally feel oppressed by the glut and mentally muddled by the clutter.

Our possessions also have an impact individually. We are reminded, often on an unconscious level, of a theme in our life every time our eyes glance at an object. I don't want to be melodramatic about this. No one ever need be afraid of any thing. Fear is not a Divine law. It is possible to possess at times a serenity that remains untouched by the influences I am speaking of. Still, our household environment, if it's not simple and free of obvious concerns, can be like a mild allergen that affects us whenever our immunity has been lowered. Therefore this aspect of our life should be adjusted to interfere as little as possible with our mental comfort. In that regard, here are a few guidelines that many people find helpful.

Spring Cleaning the Mind

When embarking on a broad external change, it is a good overall rule to begin with the smallest and easiest steps.

- Sit quietly in your least important room. If you have only one or two rooms, perhaps begin inside your car, in front of your refrigerator, or at your locker or desk in the building where you work.

- Slowly look around. Look at what is behind you, under you, above you. Try hard to take in each thing you see without adding a single judgment or criticism to it. Look at this room as if you were a stranger to it, and see it, really *see* it, for the first time.

- Relaxed, and with your eyes now closed, take in the *atmosphere* around you. How does this room *feel* to you? Do certain areas feel congested? Does some part need cleaning? Is there an unhappiness or sadness around a particular object? Is something being neglected? Are there places that seem comfortable or bright with welcome?

- Repeat these steps within a second room. Pay particular attention to any desire you have to alter the room—to clean it, throw something out, make repairs, add things to it. When you notice an urge of this sort, try describing it in detail ("My impulse is to pull up this dirty old carpet and burn it.").

This little exercise is not meant to make you paranoid about the rooms you were in or harden your judgments against certain objects. Nor is it meant to catapult you into a flurry of changes. It's difficult to learn that our observations do not require automatic action. We are accustomed to converting every insight into behavior, whereas no change need be made until we are clear within ourselves that the change will add to our mental stability. Until we are certain, possibly it is best to wait calmly. Every ambiguous action causes a disturbed aftermath. Likewise, to withdraw or become slovenly is not a solution because inaction, if motivated by fear, also has its disrupting consequences.

- Close your eyes and imagine undertaking just one of the alterations that seems feasible. Project into the future what things will be like as you make the change and after you complete the change. As best you can, see everyone and everything this will affect. Don't worry whether your fantasy is accurate, for of course it is not. Your aim is not prediction; rather it is to undergo a mental process that allows you to see how peaceful you are *now* about making this change.

- With your eyes closed, fantasize *not* making the change. Imagine the ramifications that might flow from not acting.

- Now quietly ask yourself what is your peaceful preference, what is it you want to do as of now.

- If you would like another visual way of learning whether you prefer making this particular change to the room, here are two more possibilities. Think of peace as light and, with eyes closed, observe which alternative seems "brighter" to you. Or picture yourself standing between the two alternatives and watch your body lean in the direction of your more peaceful inclination. Say to yourself, "If my purpose is to be happy, which way do I lean?" Or you can physically stand up and do this.

You may have noticed that this exercise did not concern itself with the question of whether the contemplated change to the room was "right." Issues of right and wrong can almost never be resolved without residual conflict because the grounds on which they are made shift constantly. Is it financially right? Conveniently right? Aesthetically right? Conventionally right? Is it right according to a particular book—but which passage in the book? Is it right for your spouse but not for you? Is it safe? Is it proper? And on and on. There is clearly no clarity in "right." But it is quite simple to recognize our peaceful preference.

- Repeat these steps in the remaining rooms of your house, place of work, or any other areas that contain your personal items. Perhaps make only one change in each area at this time. If in order to have a clear idea of what you are feeling in each of these locations you need to break the area into smaller units (closets, drawers, the freezer, the glove compartment), then take the time to do this.

A project such as the one suggested in this exercise, if done adequately, could take a long time, and there is nothing lost in giving yourself that time. Do only as much each day as you feel comfortable doing, and do not get caught up in the excitement of some potential change. In itself the change of throwing things out is no more conducive to our mental well-being than the change of acquiring still more.

Once you have mentally wrapped yourself around your array of possessions—clothes, food stock, tools, pictures, books, toilet items, accumulated mail—and know what emotions you have about them—not only individually but also how you feel about the quantity of things you own and how they are arranged and cared for—you are now ready to begin imposing on them your sense of simplicity.

As mentioned before, it's good to begin with the least important area and gradually work up to those rooms or places that seem more complex and evoke greater anxiety. Another helpful procedure might be to work on one area until you feel it is complete before going to the next.

- Sit quietly in the place where you have decided to begin. Look at it honestly. Drink in the atmosphere around you. Be aware of areas or items that disturb you. Then consider the first possession, which, if possible, should be one you do not care a great deal about. Look calmly at this item and ask yourself the following questions:

  "Do I still use this?" (as a decoration, a tool, a symbol of certain memories)

  "Am I still taking care of this?" (dusting it, servicing it, polishing it)

  "If I am neither caring for it nor using it, in what specific ways do I fear letting it go?" ("I may use it someday." "I might offend the one who gave it to me." "It's costly and I don't see how I will ever recoup its value.")

- If after answering these you are still unsure about whether to keep this particular possession, close your eyes and project into the future both keeping it and not keeping it. "What would life be like without this tomorrow? The next day? The next week?" And so on. Then: "What would life be like with this still here tomorrow, the next day...?"

- Now ask yourself, "Which course of action will add most to my *present* peace?" One scenario will seem more peaceful than the other.

The answer you get will not guarantee that in days to come your ego will be happy about the decision you make today. Yet isn't it clear by now that it's our fear of the future that has caused us to hang on to so many things we truly don't want?

To become consistently happy we must learn to trust our present sense of peace more than the dictates of our anxieties. Buying sprees, over-accumulation, clutter, chronic disorganization, and such are the result of consistently making decisions on the grounds of fear. A peaceful approach to life will not eliminate all mistakes in the terms we usually judge mistakes—for example, you might throw out something that later you wished you hadn't—but a peaceful approach will allow you to be happier now, and now never goes away.

Although it takes a sustained effort to form the habit of listening for and choosing our peaceful inclinations in all matters, this strength of mind is indeed within reach. The prerequisite is the recognition that it is desirable. Exercises such as this, in which the benefits of an imposed harmony can plainly be seen, give weight to an alternative to chaos.

It is not enough to see that our ongoing mental patterns are hurting us. An experience is needed to spark our belief in the existence of another way. That is why something so seemingly minor as bringing a degree of peace and order to our physical surroundings can become a rallying point for further extensions into more complex areas such as relationships. If it can be seen that love is a possibility *anywhere*, even in reorganizing a room in a gentle and self-caring way, then the journey to the deeper realms of love has begun.

CHAPTER

14

BODY

Seeing the Body Honestly

There is a limit to what the body can give us. Yet what we demand of it appears to have no bounds. We look to our body and to our relationships with other bodies for our sense of happiness perhaps more than we look to anything else "on earth and in heaven." When the performance of our body fails to meet our need "to be some-body," as inevitably it must, often our last resort is to have children, or lots of friends, or employees, or supporters, or bodies in some other role that we expect to materialize our dreams.

Most relationships, even those with our partner or child, cannot withstand this pressure and fall away beneath the weight of what we expect from them. The leading cause of relationship failure is pressure. And pressure, whether on our own body to perform or on other bodies to deliver, comes from the belief that we can get something we don't have from a body. Yet whether our focus is on our own body or on bodies in the form of relationships, we misplace our trust. Although we don't realize it at the time, this makes a loss of happiness inevitable.

As many have pointed out, the world's present preoccupation with the body approaches hysteria. To borrow from Milton, it has reached a state of "demonic frenzy, moping melancholy, and moon-struck madness." Thin bodies, young bodies, "ripped" bodies, bodies with lots of hair (in the right places), bodies with super energy, bodies with glorious tans, bodies that look presidential, bodies that never show their age, bodies that can run impressive distances.... This blur of images held up in acclaim before the public eye has created an almost complete sense of unreality about a very ordinary and not so endurable piece of machinery. Something everyone owns and almost no one can see. Very simply, we have made ourselves too afraid to look.

By cultivating impossible physical ideals we are left paralyzed in dismay at our own hopelessly inadequate anatomy or, perhaps even worse, have sent ourselves racing blindly after some fleeting physical prize that multiplies and scatters as we approach it. Understandably we do not want to look at how our own body matches up. And so we don't look at all. We truly don't need to be engrossed in all this madness, for it is irrelevant to happiness, or being deeply loved, or anything else of enduring value. It is irrelevant even to feeling good. All we need is to recognize that our body *can* become our friend, but in order for it to assume this role, we must first see it as it is.

But what horrors might we face if we took an honest look? That our mouth size makes our smile insincere? That our inherited metabolism shortens our life span? That our voice is too high for us to be promoted? That the sport we have mastered is not cardiovascularly balanced? Or possibly that our body has suddenly gone out of style—for don't we observe that "refined" facial features are admired, only to give way a few years later to faces with "more character"? One moment the hair is to be wavy and of uniform color, next it must look naturally blond and straight, then overnight it should seem genetically unruly and have sunshine highlights. At present we must lose not 5 but 25 pounds. And even if we manage that, the bone structure of our legs and pelvis is all wrong, and we don't look thin enough from a distance, even though up close we are patently anemic.

Perhaps more anxiety provoking still is the current emphasis on super-health, which when added to the evidence we see daily that it's hard enough just staying alive, results not too surprisingly in our thinking of our body as a walking time bomb, or at least as a time-consuming reclamation project stretching drearily into the future.

Obviously the body is currently an unhappy subject. Not only must we keep pace with the world's ever-shifting ideal of attractiveness, desirable personality mannerisms, and meaningful physical attainments, but also the stream of new and vital "facts" about the ways our body can torture and attack us has become a torrent that has thrown every breath, bite, and atmospheric vibration into question.

We are told that our race subjects us to high blood pressure or skin cancer, our sex to breast or prostate tumors, our age to whooping cough or stroke, our evenings out to car accidents, our job to lung disease, our exercise to back pain, and our play to bad knees. And we are informed that the most reliable remedies for these problems are themselves risky.

At a glance it certainly might seem best just to leave our two-legged tangle of disappointments and dangers completely out of mind. Unfortunately, we can't separate ourselves from our own perception of our body. Our attempts to do so merely keep the dynamics of our discomfort in the shadows so that any real improvement remains out of the question.

The Changeable Body

The body can't be perfected, but it can be changed. Its change-ableness is its fundamental characteristic and the dominant role it plays in our lives. So if you are overweight and out of shape, your body is changeable. And if you are in the bloom of youthful loveliness, your body is changeable. It will not remain the same whether you are lethargic, droopy, and prepubescent or have great upper-body strength for your age and are presently graying distinguishingly at the temples. You may play a part in its future course or not, but nothing you do or neglect to do will anchor your body in permanence. If the body lacks value, this attribute is one obvious reason. Yet it is also the body's changeableness that allows for hope no matter how much of a plague upon our mind some bodily condition has become.

Changeableness is not desirable, nor need it be resisted. But it will most certainly be feared until the ancient human habit of longing sadly for what once was, or of trying to fend off an imagined future, is finally broken. People go through old photos and think that is how their body should still be. But does anyone *really* want to be ninety and look eighteen, the only person whose body never changes, a phenomenon unique in the world to be feared and stared at? Of course the answer is "No."

Yet we persist in believing that because a particular stage was more attractive, more commanding of respect, more employable, and the like, it was therefore good and right—which makes our present state wrong. Good and right to have the advantage? How very unhappy is this attitude. The period in which the body can have all possible benefits is quite short indeed, and to try to freeze it in time is disastrous to mental well-being.

Perhaps the old photos show us obese or seriously ill. Then it will not be the past we regret losing but the future we dread.

To even consider our body at all makes us unhappy because of this fear it brings up that something might return. But the body's future is not made more secure by our dwelling on its previous stages. It is cared for best when we know it well as it now is and remain sensitive to its present needs.

The body we have at this moment is the only body we have. It was not nor will it be again what it is now. Our present body is the one we must finally come to terms with if we are ever to make this part of our world comfortable. We simply don't *have* the body of five years ago. But undoubtedly we are still reacting to those old images as if they were flesh and blood. This is hurting our health, our energy, our appearance, our moods, and a hundred other bodily aspects that have a history of influencing our happiness.

Seeing Through the Eyes of a Friend

I want you to try a rather silly exercise.

- I want you to take off your clothes and stand in front of a mirror.

- And I want you to look at your body just as it is. Don't judge it. Don't recall how it once was or tell yourself that there will soon be more of "that." See your body as one who truly loves you might see it, with kind and gentle eyes. See it in the present.

- After having a good long look, close your eyes and begin taking inventory of your state of comfort. As you stand there, how does the body feel? Are there any places where the body hurts? Is there something that is not easy to live with? Are there recurring problems with certain parts? You are not looking for areas of pride or shame because right now you are simply sensing the details of its present state.

You wish to acknowledge the overall well-being and comfort of your body and identify the particular areas of trouble that keep cropping up. Take note of anything that keeps getting your attention (the thighs, something about the digestion, an overall sense of deterioration and neglect, the back). There are of course other preoccupations that are always shifting. It's the hair one day, the eyes the next, the stomach, the posture, the wrinkles, and so on. But if you take a calm overview, you should have little trouble recognizing the areas that represent a sustained disturbance to your happiness.

Regard your body peacefully and sanely. Do not let your mind fall into its old, nagging preoccupations. "Are the pouches on my hips too unsightly?" "Is my bone structure good?" "Should my eyes be some other color or further apart?" "Am I too thin in places?" If you begin this kind of critiquing, which a good friend would not do, you soon will be unable to form the dispassionate picture you need as a starting point.

- Now sit or stand quietly for a moment and let this gentle and truthful picture of your body sink in. Remind yourself of the pointlessness of fighting the simple facts. This is merely your body. It is certainly not all there is to you, but for now this is what you have physically. You can live with it in peace. Actually, short of being in a state of chronic pain, you can live quite comfortably and happily with it— if you will accept it as it is.

Accepting your body doesn't mean that you refuse to take steps that would help you feel more at ease within it, whether this entails an operation, enrolling in a diet center, scheduling a daily workout, or having your hair styled. If you do not judge your body and are not afraid to hear your own counsel without first gathering numerous other opinions, you will sense what could help.

There is something in you that knows. Start by practicing acceptance, and follow by practicing trust. Practice knowing and you will know. Only comparisons and judgments block this thoroughly natural process. It's an indication of our culture's current disorientation that this point would even need emphasizing. What could be more natural than for one to have a gentle sense of how to care for one's own body?

- After you have surveyed your body in a mirror and in your mind's eyes, take up one of the more chronic problems and look at it with your peaceful mind.

- Proceed in the usual way of opening yourself up to all options and choosing some first step to try.

- Plan out a small program for putting this particular distress behind you. Without unnecessary soul searching and worry, simply begin implementing it. Prove to yourself that it's not necessary to remain mired in *any* form of unhappiness.

The Purpose of the Body

In most people's lives the body functions as a background noise of varying unpleasantness—an anxiety, a burden, a source of regret. At first the body seems pure promise, a bright comet racing across the future. And for a time, in its changeableness, it appears to move toward the fulfillment of many vague anticipations. But what we expected of it is as insatiable as it is ill defined. The body has not the resources to meet an ever-growing list of conflicting demands. Increasingly it appears to fail just when it is needed most. Thus it settles into its more permanent role, a thing to mistrust, a source of fear.

Your body should have at least one good and natural purpose—to be a servant to your happiness. It can fulfill this function well if you look at it calmly enough to see that once stripped of its adornments it is not a great and magical servant. It is humble and vulnerable and of limited talent. The current overemphasis has distorted its wonders—and its horrors—but has not succeeded in transmuting it into anything other than what it has always been.

Our body can serve our happiness by not interfering with our mind, but the purely physical doesn't have the capacity to make us happy. Individuals who think it will make them happy to get all fixed up, become extraordinary looking, and go to a party for the purpose of being seen are still confusing mental potential with physical potential.

The reserves of peace we carry into an event will determine how enjoyably we spend our time and not our muscle mass, the brand of our clothes, the height of our heels, the eminence of our name, or the pitch of our laugh. No matter how cute, severe, or "natural looking" a body may be, it simply can't manufacture the inner state of happiness. Yet most of the world operates from the opposite premise.

The somewhat shocking truth is that to present ourselves to the world in ordinary terms rather than "daring to be different" creates far fewer distractions. Dare to be ordinary and you will concentrate better. There is precious little courage involved in striving to be special, since this universal "need" is what makes the world go 'round. Or, more accurately, chase its tail. It obviously is not a need at all but a tired old love affair that has never found home.

It should be no mystery why getting a lot of attention for our good looks doesn't satisfy us. (As hard as it is for my sons to believe, I actually had a short period of good looks in my early thirties.) The attention is directed at the body not the self, and we feel somehow outside all the words and looks that swirl around us. Even though it can be very exciting, we can feel somewhat abandoned and forgotten.

Whether or not we have experienced the feeling of isolation that often accompanies good looks, it should at least be recognized that part of us remains the same whatever is occurring to the body. As the joke goes, "Inside every old man is a young man wondering what happened." Because their consciousness is the same, it's very hard for many elderly people to get used to the way others react to their old body.

Several years ago I started working on letting go of various prejudices I had about certain body types and quickly realized that it was difficult for me to look at *anyone* without feeling some degree of judgment. I decided to try an experiment. I explained what I had in mind to Gayle and asked if she would like to accompany me to Baskin-Robbins in our pickup (sufficiently battered and rundown to be inconspicuous).

We parked close to the entrance and, after getting our cones, sat in the truck and just watched people go in and out. It was summertime, business was good, and every conceivable body type was there—old and young, fat and skinny, buxom and bald, in varying skin shades, and dressed in a surprising variety of attire. As each customer emerged, I said to myself, "Is that a good body or a bad body? No, it's just a body."

What I expected was a degree of neutrality. The features of a body don't reveal what a person is at heart, and to see more clearly was all I hoped for. What did occur was unexpected. I was flooded with love for these people. I began to see how innocent we all are in our little fleshly costumes, that there is no harm in any of this, that in fact there is a certain richness, abundance, almost a blessing to the assortment of physiques that sprinkle the Earth.

After a while we backed out and started heading down Cerrillos Road toward home. In recent years the city of Santa Fe has beautified Cerrillos, but in those days it was a place of cheap motels, little shops with no parking, and fast-food franchises. You could always find grounds for agreement with a new acquaintance at a party by deploring this exception to Santa Fe's historic charm. You can imagine my surprise when in the midst of our drive home I realized I *loved* Cerrillos Road. I loved the red SALE signs painted permanently on the store windows, the cars that were being forced to back gingerly out into traffic, the motels with masonry facades and frame sides. I even loved Long John and Colonel Chicken.

Love, just like judgment, can't be confined. Whatever we turn our gaze upon is bathed in its gentle light, for love is the recognition that although the uses they are put to may be selfish, even cruel, the *things* of the world are guiltless. And our body is merely a thing. However we have used it in the past, it remains innocent and untainted. Once we put the body back into perspective and start looking at it honestly, our sensitivity to it increases and our concern and care for it becomes more constant.

Finding Our Location

This old exercise is one of my favorites. It never fails to leave me feeling a little more sane. It is not proof of anything, just a means of having an experience. We confuse so many strange and silly things with our identity, our self, that any trick we use to sort ourselves out can be an aid to our happiness.

- Sit comfortably, close your eyes, and begin slowly asking yourself, "Where am I?"

- Follow by asking yourself, "Am I in my hair?" "Am I in

my eyes?" "Am I in my head?" "Am I in my brain?" "Am I in my shoulders?" In an easy and pleasant way, continue down the body with similar questions, pausing after each one for a gentle sense of the answer. "Am I in my torso?" "Am I in my heart?" "Am I in my hips?"—and so forth, making the questions as general or detailed as you wish.

- When you have finished you will probably have an increased awareness of that part of you that is always you, regardless of age, haircuts, amputations, prostheses, brain damage, or any other bodily changes. This awareness may be quite strong.

How Do Mind and Body Relate?

In order to be happy, what role should our mind take toward our body? It certainly shouldn't be afraid of it, which is its attitude on most occasions. If you found that you were able to do the preceding exercise enjoyably, in the course of it your mind assumed its natural role of leadership.

When the body is pushed forward to receive the benefits of life, if it is our body and not our mind that must be in position to gain from our goals, we set ourselves up for inevitable loss because of the changeableness of the body. If we want our enjoyment of life to be steady and reliable we should not choose a place of reward that is inconstant. The body is innocent, it cannot help its nature, change is simply its governing law.

Whatever the body may not be, if experienced in the present it is indeed a good servant. Good servants don't have to be anxiously watched over and second-guessed, for that hurts their confidence and disturbs their performance. Certainly instructions are needed and boundaries must be set, and out of simple consideration care should be taken that their tasks do not exceed their capabilities and that they are generally pleased with the hours and working conditions. Similarly, the mind's function is to set guidelines for the body, then permit the body to do its job in peace.

It's good to seek the body's overall comfort in direct ways. A gentle, consistent discipline can add to its happiness, as well as to the mind's, because boundaries are in fact a symbol of caring. This is why such measures as working out an excellent diet and finding safe and pleasant ways to exercise usually have a lifting effect on one's attitude and outlook.

What hours do you keep? What kind of bed do you sleep on? Should you now wear gloves to do the dishes? Is there a better shoe? The reason we are reluctant to take the time or spend the money for improvements that would obviously make our body feel better is that we have the odd belief that because we are not consistent we don't deserve good treatment. Yet most of us find it more difficult to be kind when our body is disturbing us, and without kindness there is no happiness. You will think more gently of yourself as well as be a better friend to your partner, children, and everyone else if you act *as* if you are worthy of your own love.

Superiority Is Not Self-Caring

Unlike self-caring, superiority, conceit, arrogance, and self-importance must be protected at all costs. Kindness toward ourselves can give way to kindness toward another if need be. Most parents would sacrifice their lives for their child. But if I believe I am superior, I equate self-sacrifice with self-destruction. Kind, generous people are weak and stupid in my eyes. And if I think I am more important than others, I will consciously or unconsciously work to make others less important than me. They must be marginalized, discounted, put down, defeated, or destroyed.

The most destructive individuals I have run across in my life invariably thought they were superior.

The mindset that leads us into feelings of superiority is our desire to rank. And it begins with the body. Does it look right? Does it smell right? Is it thanked adequately? Does it get the best seat? Ranking our body reverses the natural roles of the body and mind, and the mind ceases to function as a calm overseer.

Have you noticed how some drivers speed up just a little when you start to pass them on the highway? Several years back the four of us took a vacation in a rented 20-foot RV that could do everything except accelerate. This slight increase in speed on the part of the car you are trying to pass becomes very noticeable when you are the size of a small house and in the wrong lane. Why do people suddenly go faster than they want to? Why do they break line at ticket counters, need more service than others at restaurants, and, Gayle tells me, rush into the beauty parlor unannounced for a "quick comb-out" while you are left sitting there with perm solution collecting precariously on your eyebrows? It's because of the undue self-importance they assign to their body, which is where self-importance must be assigned since the mind doesn't exist on the level of these petty competitions.

The purpose of the body is to not give the mind reason to be distracted. And the purpose of the mind is to not constantly worry whether the body is receiving everything that is its due. The usual alliance of fear gives way to harmony when the mind leads in certainty and the body follows in peace. For this to happen, the body must be treated and thought of gently.

CHAPTER

15

HEALTH

A Happy Balance

Extremes in food, clothing, exercise, facial appearance, health, or safety can sometimes disturb the basic friendliness and compatibility of the body and turn it into an annoyance. But a middle road can be walked whereby the body is comfortable in most respects and thus is not a preoccupation.

The body is best clothed comfortably but not distractingly. It is best fed so that its well-being is enhanced and protected, yet not so restricted that it is imbued with sacrifice and deprivation, which are themselves indisposing. It is unhappy to over-adorn the body, yet to neglect its appearance so that it becomes unpleasant to look at is equally unhappy. Letting the body go brings no true relief to the mind, nor is it satisfying to try to push it to enviable levels of health and energy. Furthermore, the body's safety should not be neglected in the name of a spiritual path or to demonstrate trust in God. On the other hand, to become fanatical about avoiding all conceivable mishaps is simply a miserable way to live.

To guide our body in a balanced, reasonable way is difficult in the present climate in which people are taking extreme stands on every possible bodily issue. When Shrikrishna Kashyap first came to this country to practice Ayurveda, a woman came to him with a mild stomach disorder, and he suggested that she drink a little dill-seed tea each day. When she came back two weeks later, he asked how she was doing. "I'm afraid there hasn't been much improvement. My stomach isn't feeling so good." He was surprised to hear this. "Have you been taking the dill-seed tea every day?" "Oh yes," she replied. "Well then, tell me what else your diet consists of." "Oh nothing else!" she assured him. "I've been drinking only the dill-seed tea."

With this as the general approach to life surrounding you, you want to stay alert to any tendency you feel to go to extremes. Gently decline to be influenced, and return instead to your own natural intelligence. It is possible for example to discover for yourself what combination of foods makes your body happy, gives it stamina, and allows it to sleep well. And also what saps its energy, lowers its resistance, or stirs it up in some disagreeable way. If you will go about this sensibly and not rush the process, you can come to have a confident sense of what to eat and how to eat it. So too is it possible to develop a pleasant and sure instinct of what to wear, when to use makeup and other aids to appearance, how and when to exercise, what to do when ill, and which allowances to make for your age.

We must not underestimate our resistance to this. The "normal" tendency is to fluctuate between extremes—rigidly punishing the body on one hand and giving up on it on the other.

The happiest body is the one that does not stand out in either a negative or a positive way. It is a body that is comfortable with itself, as well as comfortable to look at. Even a very elderly body can be gentle on the mind and on the eye if the mind that inhabits that body is at ease with the body's age and physical state. As we develop a loving sensitivity to our highly individual constitution, we become accepting of its changes, even of its illnesses and injuries, and also of the diminishing capacities that accompany advancing years.

It is possible to be sick in peace, have one's period in peace, experience menopause in peace, grow bald in peace, become less sexually arousable in peace, and be quite old and withered in peace. The time will arrive when you will look in the mirror and know that the call to be the centerfold will never come. And that very afternoon you may be warmly praised by some member of the younger generation for making it up the post office steps. None of this *has* to cause anguish, but for it not to we first need to be at home with our body so that its changes in appearance and physical capacity are not feared or denied.

The Body as Pet

There is now a trend, some of it within the body-mind-spirit movement, to identify *less* with the body. Unfortunately this often has the reverse effect of what we desire. Instead of increasing communication with our deeper self and bringing into sharper focus the part of us that is not always changing, it tends to confuse our sense of identity and sets up little wars within our mind. Even from a metaphysical standpoint, until individuals "awaken" or ascend, the body is part of their mind. Thus it's unlikely that the mind can remain peaceful while denying what the body needs.

The key to a happy, healthy body is to treat it like a beloved pet. If we project our moods onto our pets, as we so often do with our body, we respond to them inappropriately. But if we look closely at our pets and identify with what they are feeling, we are a comfort to them, and they in turn are little gifts of affection and funniness to us.

Most of us have a more balanced sense of how to identify with a dog than with a body. We love our dog today, but we can't love our body because we are waiting for it to be different. By not being apprehensive about our dog, we give him the gift of seeing him as he is. We know that on summer nights he likes to be in the fenced backyard where he can practice defending us in his highly vocal way, without worry of being confronted by another dog. Perhaps in winter we put him up at night on an old blanket in the corner of the kitchen. We don't wash his bedding too often because we know that he likes things that are well worn and have a familiar smell. Neither do we insist that he sleep on the king-size bed while we take the couch. This would distress him greatly, and he might end up on top of us, licking our face and asking for forgiveness.

We are acquainted not only with his pleasures but also the diameters of his health and constitution. So we feed him a good but simple diet. We don't scrape just anything into his bowl, nor do we thaw out every cut of meat in the freezer and pile it around him just because he would think this very exciting. We know that these kinds of indulgences would make him sick.

We recognize that a few "No's" keep him happy and safe. So we keep him off the street and far from skunks and porcupines. We exercise him and bathe him and take him to get his shots. And we do not expect him to understand why or to feel like obeying all instructions. There is no real war in this relationship because there is neither neglect nor a battle for perfection. He is just a dog, and he is our dog, and so we love him and guide him and treat him fairly. In return he is our innocent friend and harmless companion. And as long as we have it, why must our body be anything less? Therefore, when we have a question about what to do or not do for our body, a helpful exercise is simply to ask, "If my body were a beloved pet, what would I do?"

It Is Innocent to Be Sick

As a culture, our definition of what it means to be sick has become increasingly arbitrary. This is a reflection of our tendency either to denigrate or to romanticize the body. Having a cold or flu is being sick, but to be unhappy or afraid is not. Loss of bone mass from radiation received at work is an illness, but damaged legs and hips from skiing or jogging is not. I was once at a party and a man who rode a "Hog" (Harley-Davidson) saw the bandage on my forehead and asked if it was a dirt-bike injury. "No," I said, "I had a small growth removed." I watched his estimate of my character instantly plummet.

It is unnatural for one to be sick because sickness itself is looked at as unnatural. Anger, on the other hand, which can resemble an asthma attack, is often treated as a sign of courage and self-respect. Somehow the illness, whatever it is, should not be happening to us. Even though we live in a world of sickness, we should not be sick. If we are, someone is to blame. Maybe a friend was negligent while contagious. Maybe we somehow "chose" the illness. Maybe someone in our life is a negative influence. Maybe it's the fault of the FDA, AMA, dairy lobby, beef lobby, pharmaceutical industry—we can never settle on where to place blame permanently. We are certain of one thing only: Blame must be placed.

Small wonder that we narrow so absurdly what we call sickness and that when we can no longer escape even our own arbitrary definitions, we try to run away from our sick body and out from under the time of our sickness: "When will this be over?" "Why did this happen to me?" In the course of thinking these thoughts, we once again do not look at our body. We mentally avoid it and deny it and never wholeheartedly give it time to rest and heal.

Once, when Jordan was sixteen months old, he had a typical reaction to his last measles-mumps-rubella shot. At the same time John, then five years old, had a mild case of flu. Some of our friends thought that Gayle and I were to blame for John's condition because two days before we had taken him to a birthday party even though it was the height of flu season. Some other friends believed we were the cause of Jordan feeling bad.

There are authorities and their followers who advocate never giving certain shots to children, as well as those who say always give them. More often than not both sides believe that any who do not do as they warn deserve the consequences. Not surprisingly they are secretly glad when the child gets sick because this appears to prove their position.

These are miserable lines of thought that Gayle and I have tried to avoid by refusing either to defend our position or to urge it on others. The truth was that we didn't know. Who really does? So we admitted this to ourselves and made the best choice for our kids that we could. All parents have available to them a peaceful preference about what to do at the moment. This they can feel when they dwell on their love for their child rather than on their many noisy fears of making a mistake.

Earlier I said, "Practice knowing and you will know." It is good to distinguish between the knowing that comes from fear verses the knowing that comes from peace. Much of the world's unhappiness results from lumping them together. We can always know what we *believe* in the present, and this form of knowing can be practiced until it becomes a calm, steady assurance. Gayle and I didn't know what the results of the birthday party or the shot would be in advance, but we sat quietly long enough to discover what we *believed* was the most loving option for each child.

Faced with a decision, most people's desire is to see their way through. But that blocks their present knowledge of what they believe. We naturally wish to protect ourselves from making a mistake. But mistakes—as the world usually perceives them—do not truly matter within the present. They are an interpretation of something that will come later.

Remember that your goal is happiness and that this state is composed of kindness never delayed but exercised always in the present. Happiness isn't what merely looks kind but what feels kind in our heart. You cannot seek to be perceived as right by the world and at the same time be gentle to yourself and others, because these goals apply to different times. You can be right in the future, but you can only be kind now.

Kindness toward children is the same as toward relatives, friends, and strangers. It is the touching of hearts, the acknowledgment and embracing of connection. It is the gesture of the inner spirit and as such cannot be judged by the future. In the case of the birthday party and shot, the one factor that we had in hand was our love for our children. We worked hard to make this factor the deciding one, and despite the criticism we received, we noticed that both our children were happy, even though they were also sick.

Being Sick Naturally

Frequently children are sick more happily than adults because they don't get entangled in guilt, panic, blame, worry, and other irrelevant emotions. They are simply sick. Jordan and John would no more have thought of faulting themselves or us for their symptoms than it would have occurred to them to assign guilt to being out of breath from running, feeling groggy at night, having weak arms after carrying a heavy load, experiencing chills from certain noises, being blinded by bright lights, or any other symptoms of bodily limitations accepted by the world as "perfectly healthy." They had not yet made illness an unnatural part of life. Consequently their minds were relaxed enough to adjust to it when it came. Being at ease with an illness, provided it is not physically devastating or life threatening, is also an attainable state for most adults.

Most of us see nothing unnatural about our body being temporarily younger, stronger, more smooth-complexioned, or more eye-catching than other bodies. We don't feel compelled to conceal these disparities. Yet we are embarrassed to call in sick! In contrast, most little children think nothing of stopping abruptly in the middle of play and telling their playmates, "I have to sit down now, I have a tummy ache." As yet they have no silly healthier-than-thou self-image to uphold.

Children are also happier because they don't use illness as a time for soul-searching. We who are supposedly wiser believe we must find significance in the way we get sick. Before they run off, his playmates don't counsel the child with the tummy ache to work on his unwillingness to digest new situations. Yet let the modern adult get sick and they feel they must torture themselves with books, articles, and snatches of conversation that relate infirmities to character traits and behaviors. No longer do people have simple constipation—they are now tagged as emotionally repressed. Gallstones point to latent hostility. Sore throats mean you're uncommunicative. And lower back pain is fear of money (I kid you not, I can show you the book).

Certainly there could be such connections in individual cases, but isn't it obvious that these formulas are so generalized as to be meaningless? And what real purpose do they serve? I heard another one a while back. A friend went to a seminar and told me the speaker said that cancer was an inability to love. In my work I have known many cancer patients, and this statement is completely untrue. Is it realistic to think that the promulgation of such a concept will result in cancer patients becoming more loving people? Will it deepen the bond between them and their nurses, therapists, and doctors? Will it add to their peace and lessen their misery?

When we get sick there is at least one lesson we should learn from children. Little kids don't mark time. They settle into the moment at hand. An illness is often no more than our body's way of calling for a halt, calling for rest. Provided your work or parenting demands allow, do the things and take the remedies that will make this one day a little easier. If this means bed and a good book, let it be this without guilt. Ask not why it started. Have no interest in when it will be over. Set no goals that put you at odds with your condition. As best you can, remain sick in the present.

The unhappy part of our mind is always trying to get us to do what we do not need to be doing now. If we are ill, it's always best to cut back on everything we can and arrange the situation so we can be as comfortable as possible. Often there is someone who would be glad to help us out, in fact they would feel loved by being asked. Trading away our peace of mind to save ourselves the temporary embarrassment of asking for help is a poor bargain.

Nor do we demonstrate more character by turning down medicine or a trip to the doctor. Since many people now believe that taking medicine is a spiritual or moral failure, when they do succumb, they tend to overdose themselves, trying to eradicate every telltale symptom of the shameful state. Do not carry on as if you were not sick. This is arrogant, not noble. So don't become alarmed and begin chasing about for a silver-bullet remedy or try to shake the illness as if it somehow could be ducked from under. Be honest with yourself quickly. You are sick. Then resolve to be thoughtful and generous to your body.

Life-Threatening Illness

Very often when people learn that they have a life-threatening illness they become profoundly confused, and sometimes even physically disoriented, because they unconsciously believe that they have been singled out for special punishment. Quite naturally, they do not understand. The disease appears to have picked them out from thousands, and there seems to be no sound reason why they were selected.

And indeed there is no reason, and no authority or book has ever succeeded in making it completely and finally understandable to anyone. If it were genuinely understandable it would also be reasonable, and in what conceivable way is it reasonable to find yourself in pain and dying of a disease?

Although people with a life-threatening illness cannot be expected to recognize this at first, we can hope that eventually they will see that to continue pursuing the question "Why me?" is to enter a dark and hopeless pit from which it can take a long time to pull themselves out. Any line of thought that leads inevitably to guilt is of no use to you, for it will merely increase your sense of misery and so distract and disorient you that you will not be as sensitive to needed steps as you might otherwise be. It is never helpful to "assume responsibility" in the sense of taking on blame.

Attack in any form is neither responsible nor truthful, yet criticism and guilt are frequently more prevalent in cases of life-threatening illness because of the bewilderment those involved are often thrown into. It is not more honest to blame or more humble to feel guilty. These attitudes will not relieve your mind, and they will never truly succeed in rallying your friends to draw close. So do all you can to direct your mind into more helpful channels.

Because confusion over the true cause of the illness is so

common during its early stages, those individuals affected need to get into a calm and peaceful state—as calm and peaceful as is possible—and try to see what steps they wish to take. As in all other matters, every option should be considered. If done without panic, this will bring a small measure of relief into the mind as it becomes clear that there is more than one course available.

Do not be afraid to try or not to try anything. This is your body and you are free to proceed as you choose. So look at your disease with your peaceful instincts. Freeze the situation in calmness and examine it carefully. Then open yourself to all possible alternatives and begin with whatever first steps you find are the most comfortable ones to think of taking.

It is never a good idea, and this is especially true during the period just after learning that you have a life-threatening illness, to begin indiscriminately mentioning your situation to others. Very few people can resist the urge to warn and advise. One or two people in whom you have deep confidence can be confided in, but you wish to avoid the inevitable confusion that comes from just *hearing* contradictory opinions. Do not assume that you are beyond being influenced by well-meaning people in just this way. Conflict can enter your mind almost unnoticed, and suddenly you find yourself doubting your own peaceful knowing and do not understand where your uncertainty came from.

Confusion comes from worrying about making a mistake rather than from being open to taking a step. Very often the advice one gets from relatives and friends is tainted by their quite natural anxiety and will agitate and fragment your mind rather than calm and focus it.

Follow a course that is your course. If you wish to die in peace, that is your right. If you want to try many approaches, to do everything medically and alternatively that you can, this also is your right. To first inform yourself is fine and can be a definite part of coming to your own way, but you do wish to monitor carefully your tolerance for new articles and pronouncements. Remember that these will never stop. There will never be a final announcement made on which all minds suddenly agree, so you will wish to chart your own course through all of this, taking what information illumines your way and not fearing to decline to read more once you have settled on an approach.

If you have strong confidence in a particular doctor or someone else in a position to guide you, then it is best to begin with this person and listen deeply to what is said. After you have received the counsel, take it into your heart and gently arrive at your own decision.

Frequently individuals reach a peaceful decision, but then it is thrown and tossed about in their mind, they talk about it to others, they read a new article, and very shortly they are again dismally uncertain and confused. Please observe that these bulletins, articles, chat-room statements, and so forth conflict dramatically. It is essential that you plot a course within all these opinions that is your own course, your own way. Do not be afraid to trust yourself, to think your own thoughts, and to walk gently and easily toward your goal, whether this is to go all out to heal the condition, to learn to live with it in peace, or to die in an atmosphere of your choosing. Honor your heart in all ways, and your choices will be good and kind to all.

We Are Not Alone

Fear is the great companion of all illness. There is always a tendency to withdraw into that fearful part of oneself, to shrink into a frightened little object and to be one who is alone. Plotting one's own course does not mean diving into martyrdom, loneliness, and isolation. The ego involvement we all have in illness, any illness, is always a form of withdrawal or, more precisely, a withdrawing into our unhappiness and a withdrawal of our love for others, regardless of whether our outward contact with them remains the same or is increased.

In learning to develop and trust our own instinctive knowledge of our body and what it needs, and thereby becoming less dependent on the inconsistent opinions of the world, we will actually develop a stronger rather than a diminished bond with other people. Your bond with everyone is found rather than lost within your own basic nature and knowing. Even in being less open to relatives' and friends' surface anxieties and advice, we should have a sense of joining them on this deeper level, of overlooking their fears and siding with the real love behind their gestures.

If your illness requires that you rest and be physically alone, as most illnesses do, then hold your loved ones closely to your heart. Do not let guilt over your condition, or false pride, create within you vague feelings of distance and estrangement between you and anyone, for this is never a necessary part of being sick. You will find that it is often easier to see beyond other people's weaknesses when they are not around, so take advantage of the perspective that your physical isolation affords you by resting easy with any relationship that may come to mind.

In any discussion of the body it must be remembered that if we become engrossed with how we differ from everyone else, we automatically lose sight of the deeper connections that bind us all. We can even come to believe that they don't exist. The desire for happiness, for simple peace, is a continuous stream running through the core of every person and joins us all in one unseen family. Again and again our heart calls us to come back to our love for one another, to remember our oneness, and to treat others as we would be treated.

By recalling our debt of gratitude to all who touch our life, we do more to promote our health and to lend a sense of well-being to our body than any procedure, exercise, or regimen that can be performed without love. So many of the things we do for our body are carried on as if we exist in a vacuum. This is true even within teams, exercise groups, jogging clubs, and the like, where so often there is the form of joining but not heartfelt oneness. This is a needless and sad waste.

In trying to practice oneness, it is helpful to realize that you are attempting to pass beyond the very foundation of the world's unhappiness. It is not realistic for you to expect easy and dramatic results. But a little gain now can remain with you for a very long time.

The unrelenting image that the world holds up for all to gaze upon is the image of separation—everything standing apart and no realistic hope of all hearts beating as one. Whenever we get caught up in even the most trivial of worldly problems, we instantly take its picture of reality to heart and suffer loneliness in some form. The problem cries out, "Are you separate? Are you separate?" Learn not to answer this question, for only one small obsession with the world is sufficient to "prove" that indeed you are.

A person can feel separate in a crowd, with a group of friends, even in the midst of a large family. Loneliness is not a friendless state; it is the major symptom of the world. It is the unavoidable price of taking the terrain one presently travels too seriously. The world does not work, and this still seems to surprise us. The feelings of not ever being completely understood, of having to be wary of using up other people's goodwill, of being saddled with certain relationships, of having too much to do by ourselves—these emotions are a constant and almost universal undercurrent to thought. They stem from placing great stock in how things go for us instead of how deeply rooted we are in our core. Yet if there is no real awareness of the core itself and what it implies, no other outcome can realistically be expected.

We will not first believe in a place of quiet within us and then experience it. We must have an experience first, and then another, and another, until our faith in its reliability and its locality begins to flood our mind. A distant light is dimly seen but not quite believed. Nevertheless it is walked toward. And with each step it grows brighter. There is no mystery to this process. The following exercise could be such a step.

- Once in the morning and evening, for 5 or 10 minutes, silently and slowly repeat these words: "I am gentle. I am peace. I am one."

  As you say this, try to become gradually aware of a place in you that the words point to, a place of utter stillness and peace, the one part of you where there is no loneliness and no change.

- While continuing to repeat these words, let this little spot of stillness grow. Let it expand. Watch it bloom. But do not want it to grow, and do not expect it to. You are simply focusing on a reality, and as you do so it naturally becomes more obvious. Merely experience whatever you are aware of without measuring or judging a thing.

Remember that you may not know this part of you well, so you may not be in position to calculate what it should be doing for you. What perhaps you do not yet believe is that this part of you is you. You are you, and because of that simple fact, you are not alone. Isn't it obvious that an experience is badly needed? So perhaps do this little exercise for several days.

CHAPTER 16

RELATIONSHIP

What to Expect

In no place is happiness sought more hopefully and dashed more consistently than in relationship. Still we continue to see in it our delivery from a multitude of pains. This is doubly tragic because our insight into the potential of relationship is actually well grounded. But it's as if over and over we walk into a room of extraordinary beauty and peace—our room, set aside for us, overflowing with the riches we long for—and each time come away with nothing, perplexed and angry, resolved never to try again.

Yet we don't know where else to turn. With a new relationship at least we have hope. It seems that an aging man can be renewed by a young woman. An aging woman renewed by a young man. An unhappy marriage renewed by a baby. The expectation placed on the new body—the new friend, new doctor, new boss, new spouse—is so great that soon it fails to live up to what we wanted. The doctor makes a mistake. The new friend has the wrong politics. The baby won't sleep through the night. Disillusionment gradually sets in, and soon the person must be turned away from in order for us to "keep our sanity."

It seems naive to expect this pattern ever to be reversed. But as with all dynamics, we must first see how we participate. Until our part in these little dances of doom is recognized, we will continue blaming the new body, whatever its description, for the failure this time. Then we begin running after a new relationship to save us.

What we expect of a relationship sets up initial disappointment and frequently leads to failure. We think it's only natural to have expectations, but our expectations are based on the past and are blind to the present. For example, many children want adults to give them only a narrow range of acceptable toys. When an adult doesn't know which gifts a child expects, the child can express sharp disappointment upon opening a present that isn't what she expects. The child has had fun with robots in the past, so now her first board game looks downright ugly and no fun, even though later, after giving it a try, the game might become her favorite plaything.

It is a mistake of course to turn against a present because it's not what one expected, but it's a tragic mistake to reject a person because of expectations. All expectations are a judgment, and there is no relationship, whether between a parent and child, between two couples, or between an animal and a person, that expectations will not undermine.

Along with the right toys, children expect parents to provide the perfect childhood, and children don't even know what this is or should be. As children grow older, their ideas of what is needed constantly change, and later as adults they are uncertain whether to denounce or be thankful for the conditions under which they grew up.

The expectations that parents have of their children are perhaps more conspicuous. Children should look a certain way. Definitely they should be intelligent and try hard in school. They should have many friends and be pleasing to adults as well. And so forth—whatever the values of the parents are. Even with a new baby there are souring expectations. It shouldn't hiccup too much in the womb. It should come out easily. It should be the right sex. It should sleep through the night. It should nurse or drink its little bottle well. It should not have colic or unsightly rashes.

Certainly great expectations are placed on a new friendship, and even more so if it's potentially a romantic one. The long-term relationship is highly valued by the world, although at present it is cool to be fearful and overly cautious of forming even short-term ones. Yet there is also a myth that a special few can have a lifelong union in which they stare meaningfully into each other's eyes, hang upon each other's every word, and are thrilled by each other's touch year after year. There is much pretense about this, and articles are written on how to maintain this type of relationship, how to add new "mystery" and "spice." Rules are given on ways to draw back from the other person and hold him or her spellbound and in love with you forever. The expectations thus created are very sad because they are so far off the mark that they tend to drive wedges between people who had a perfectly fine relationship until one of them was abducted by a magazine article.

An expectation is looking for something rather than looking at something. We anticipate one thing and do not clearly see the other thing that is at hand. Because what we anticipate is not there, we place a veil of mourning over all that lies beneath our gaze.

What Not to Expect

If we could but look at it and want nothing, this day could comfort us and make us glad far beyond what we expect. We expect too little when we want only another version of the past.

Discard fantasies and open your heart to the instant. This is feasible, but first you must assume that, unless you have already done the work involved, every relationship you have is to some degree obscured by what you expect of it. And expectations, like cataracts, must be removed. There is no way to see around them.

- Set aside a few minutes, and consider only one relationship. Perhaps the one receiving most of your attention from day to day.

- Mentally stand this person before you, and look carefully at everything that comes to mind. Search each thought for expectations, for how you *want* this person to be. Consider his or her body, occupation, personal mannerisms, past and present behavior, selection of friends, dress habits, state-of-the-world opinions—anything at all that you associate with this individual.

  Whenever you feel a tinge of irritation or disapproval, you can be sure that you have an underlying expectation. If, for instance, you are considering one of your parents and are recalling a recent phone call, if you remember being upset about something that was said, you must realize that you expected your mother or father to somehow be different. This could be a very long-standing expectation. The fact that people prove over and over that they are not a certain way does not lessen our wish that they were. For example, a divorce followed by years of estrangement from an ex-spouse often has very little effect on the anger felt over how he or she should have been.

- If you find it difficult to become aware of the expectations you have, you might try the Gestalt Therapy technique of pulling up a chair and then vividly picturing this individual sitting in it. With your eyes either open or closed, tell this man, woman, or child exactly what you want of it. Speak straight from your heart and hold back nothing. You can do this silently, but if that doesn't make the person seem real enough, try saying it out loud.

- When you have gotten everything off your chest, it's important that you physically get up, sit in the other individual's chair, mentally become that person in every way you can, and answer yourself back.

  Most people find it helpful to shuttle back and forth between chairs until everything has been said on both sides. You might think of this as acting out a dialogue between you and the individual. Notice that as you proceed, a gradually increasing level of understanding and sympathy develops and your initial expectations begin to weaken. Sensing that this will happen, you may feel a strong resistance to sitting in the other person's chair. This comes of course from not *wanting* to understand the other person. This exercise also shows that to have expectations of others generates in them opposing expectations of us.

- Once your expectations are identified, you must discard them from your mind so the relationship can be experienced in the present. This discarding process must not be undermined. For example, no matter what erasing technique we used, if we were to continue describing to others what we had to endure as a child, there is no conceivable way we could see our parents as they actually are today. To free our mind of expectations we must stop complaining or telling witty stories about our ex-spouse, our new supervisor, our teenager, or the family down the street. Our mind will not accept a new truth while our conversations continue to deny it.

- One simple method for relinquishing expectations is to bring the person to mind and then go down the mental list you have made, saying with each item:

"_____(Name)_____, I no longer want
_____(specific expectation)_____. I want *nothing* from you. You are free."

Say the words until you can sense that you mean them.

- Using mental imagery is another effective way of discarding expectations. One that I find helpful is to picture each expectation as a string I have tied to the other person. With a pair of golden scissors (why "golden," I don't know; feel free to use the material of your choice), I cut each attachment until the individual stands free. Since the strings we tie to a relationship always connect at both ends, we are released along with the other individual.

- If you have detected a little of the ugliness that your expectations have spread across your image of another person, you can use a visualization that strips this away. A mask or costume can be removed to reveal the basic blamelessness, if not loveliness, of the person. I am thinking of a friend whom, even though he has been this way for 25 years, I always expect not to be competitive. So I say to him now, "You are free to be competitive. You do not have to change for me to be your friend," and I picture my expectations lifting from him like a suit of unattractive armor.

Beneath the usual layers of expectations that each person carries into a relationship, there is often still another growing in strength. It is the very understandable anticipation of abandonment. The one who has been loved for so long may leave. And indeed this is the way of the world. The spouse may die or find another. The best friend may become enchanted with individuals who move in another sphere. The parent may become old and mentally withdraw into some unreachable world.

Somehow a way must be found to set aside all these sad images if we are ever to be free enough and present enough to have a real relationship with anyone. Yet it seems so unlikely that such a task could be completed because the possible distressing turns that each relationship could take are so numerous. Many teenagers do in fact turn sullen. Babies are often surprisingly demanding. A parent develops an irrational fear of impoverishment.

Of course, we can't ignore these difficult realities if they are occurring now. But one does not have to anticipate them if they are not. With all that could happen to our loved ones being shouted at us from every corner of the media, the only hope we have of partaking of the rich potential of our relationships is to want them and to have them within the present only. So often it seems that someone has to die before we realize all the opportunities we missed to be happy with this person. If only we had paused a moment and gazed at what was within our very hands.

However, ignoring the issues disturbing our enjoyment of a relationship is never called for. Although this approach is extremely common, it only allows issues to remain in place and fester. The problem does not go away, and neither does the habit of not addressing the problem. New ones are continually added to the old, until one day there is an unexplainable and permanent pall over the relationship. And it is no longer worth the effort.

Our ego's solution to this dynamic is to bring up any hint of difficulty forcefully and at once and to "attack" the problem on the spot. As a result, these frequent confrontations so valued now as signs of "being yourself" and "owning your own power" and "setting your boundaries" produce the same long-term effect as ignoring problems—the relationship is eventually turned away from.

Resolving Issues

If your partner has just done something that sets you off, this probably is not the time to bring it up, because you may not be able to do so without some element of attack. And this will only precipitate counterattack. It's worth the effort to question the value of seizing our first reaction and waving it like a red flag.

Relationship problems should be recognized as they occur but dealt with when the possibilities for cooperation are greatest. If you feel a sense of urgency, your ego is involved in some way. What harm can come from waiting for this to lessen? Your partner will also tend to react less defensively about what he or she did as time passes. Your chances of a resolution are further improved if your partner senses that you are bringing the subject up because your motive is friendship and not anger. So take a moment to think through why you are mentioning this at all. Become clear that you are seeking to strengthen the bond between you and not trying to correct an equal.

If the no-fault concept can be applied to insurance, surely there is room for it in relationships. Couples frequently spend all their goodwill and most of their time together attempting to blame and control each other. In order for an issue to be solvable, we must admit to ourselves that we have taken part in whatever has occurred. This procedure shows our mind the necessity of joining with our partner to solve a mutual difficulty. Simply recognize that each person plays a role in any disturbance. If this were not so we would not feel disturbed.

Participation is not always overt. Very often one person is merely acting out what both individuals are feeling. Among the most common and disrupting relationship problems is some undermining doubt that circulates in one of the party's minds. Within a marriage, for instance, as long as one spouse dwells on the question "Should I get a divorce?" there is no hope of commitment, and you can be certain that the lack of it is always felt by the other.

When the question of whether or not to leave is present, the tendency of the mind is to gather evidence against the partner rather than to try to make the relationship work. Gathering evidence blinds us to innocence, and so a way must be found to put aside, at least temporarily, the question "Should I be in this relationship?" Or the other question friends or relatives love to plant when they say, "You can do better than (this person)."

A simple device such as completely committing oneself to the marriage for one week, one month, or one year at a time can give it a chance to breathe and show its potential. Anyone is capable of answering the question "Do I want to take the first step toward a divorce *today*?" If you see that at present you have no such wish, then try hard to have the best marriage possible for this entire day.

How to Argue in Peace

If a relationship is to avoid being crushed by the weight of its unanswered issues, a way must be found to eliminate them as they arise. We have already reviewed some prerequisites to attempting a resolution—being aware of our expectations, releasing the mind of fundamental doubts about the relationship itself, recognizing our own participation in the problem at hand, and waiting for a good time to bring the matter up—but once these conditions have been met, how can two people put a disagreement peacefully and permanently behind them?

An issue can appear solved, but because one person intimidated, cajoled, nagged, or reasoned the other into compliance, and because the one who complied was not sincere, a residue of resentment remains. Although there may now be surface agreement, the relationship has not been helped.

The means for correct resolution of an issue are always the same: The individuals must bypass their separate ego positions and unite. What form this takes does not matter, but in most cases, without some outward form, the process is never quite completed. By breaking a disagreement into its separate parts and arguing it out in a more formalized way, the mind can concentrate better and the heart has time to be heard.

Even in the worst altercations there are good moments—but they come at the wrong time. Our habit is to express our second thoughts and goodwill when they are most likely to be batted down. When the following ten steps are applied, they tend to sort out the jumble of pieces that make up an unsuccessful argument and put them into a workable whole.

1. *Deal only with the present.* The relationship may have already grown past the problems you keep recalling, so wait until an issue has genuinely entered the present. Simply because you are unhappy, do not dredge up old injuries. Remember that the relationship itself is always an easy target. Take the relationship as it is today. See the *relationship* and not its history. Do not endlessly discuss its problems and cherish them as part of its identity. Do not analyze the relationship. If there are no problems, don't think of any. Enjoy each other now, for this is the reason you are together.

2. *If something comes between you*—and it has if even one person thinks it has—*sit down together as soon as practical.* What your

bodies do symbolizes your priorities. Thus to discuss a subject on which there is a difference of opinion while doing something else (fixing dinner, driving, making love, eating) tends to deepen the conflict. If either of you is angry, both of you should first calm your minds before talking. Sit down together and quietly remember your purpose. Of course, for one of you to pressure the other into doing any of this will defeat your aim.

3. *One at a time, state your ego position in as much detail as you wish*, but do not justify it or argue its correctness. Describe your stance in complete honesty and openness, but do not attack your partner's stance.

4. *Do not interrupt, and do not call each other on breaking these guidelines.* Your aim is to join in peace, and you do not want to needlessly stir up your partner's resistance by listing faults or calling attention to mistakes.

5. *Deal only with the issue at hand.* Avoid the inclination to lump together so many problems that resolution becomes impossible. Do not try to think of causes or connections. Do not bring up the past at all unless you are absolutely sure this will add to the chances of resolution.

6. *State your position again, only this time, instead of saying what you want, say what you are afraid of.* You will always be willing to let go of a fear, once you see it as fear, but you will be tempted to feel resentful and deprived when you consider compromising on what you think you *want*. And your partner's fears will be more understandable to you than his or her demands or accusations. There is always fear behind these issues. They always symbolize something we are afraid of.

7. *While your partner is talking, truly listen.* Repeat to yourself, "_____(Name)_____ really means this." There is a tendency for couples to think that their partner's stance is pretense or that they have a hidden agenda—because they are so obviously wrong. Respect is not earned, it is given. Unless you take this person seriously you have no hope of uniting with an equal.

8. *Close your eyes and remember your debt of gratitude to your partner.* Be willing to use any mental trick that allows you to see what your partner means to you. Perhaps remember when you first met. Or maybe list to yourself any recent signs of the other's thoughtfulness, gentleness, or patience. Although this can be done silently, Gayle and I often make this a game. Taking turns, we cite ten instances of the other's goodness, cuteness, or desirability. When you are angry you can't think of a single redeeming quality, especially one you are going to have to say out loud. So if you play this, remember that the first few may be hard to think of, but if you persist, you will loosen up and the others will come more easily.

9. *With your eyes still closed, decide on three gifts you want to give the relationship.* Earlier you would have thought of these as compromises or concessions, but if you did step 8, such an interpretation is now impossible. Make sure that your gifts relate directly to the issue being resolved and truly serve to narrow the distance between you. Do not make grand off-the-subject gestures. Simply think of a few specifics that are within your present ability to carry out happily. And make them genuine gifts that you know your partner will appreciate.

10. *Open your eyes and, in turn, verbally share your gifts.* There will now be more than enough flexibility to resolve the argument.

Maybe it will be seen as a non-issue by both. Maybe one of you will recognize that you do not feel strongly, and the fact that the other *does* is all the reason you need to want the same. Maybe new options will have been thought of. Maybe the accommodations you both make will split the difference between you. If not, repeat the steps or perhaps just live happily with the effort made for a while until you both feel ready to try again.

Our Sabotaging Ways

People who don't have a relationship long to have one. People who are in one long to be free. When it comes to our own happiness, it takes a lot of honesty to admit just how perverse we are.

For example, many of the questions that keep a relationship stirred up are unanswerable at the time the mind is reviewing them:

"Will my husband die before I do?"

"Is my wife capable of having an affair?"

"Will adolescence mark the end of this closeness with my child?"

There is simply no way for a relationship to attain its lovely potential while questions of this sort are in the background.

Unhappy questions like these are not put to rest by being answered because no final answers exist. Therefore the questions themselves must be seen for what they are—the fear of being happy—and discarded. This is not easy, but we *are* free to choose not to consider seriously any question from our ego.

The ego part of us does not want relationship—any relationship—to endure. Union of any sort threatens its sense of autonomy. To our ego, value lies in being different, so for us to strive to have no real differences with our partner seems self-destructive.

In our counseling Gayle and I have seen hundreds of examples of people switching sides just to keep a fight going. "You are never upset for the reason you think," says *A Course in Miracles.* Our ego is upset because upset prevents joining, and it guesses correctly that joining will be the death of it.

Being right is our primary way of being different. And it always yields a feeling of distance and estrangement. The remedy is to recognize our far deeper desire for closeness and oneness and to use our considerable understanding of the other person, first, to avoid unnecessary rifts and second, to do only what will be *received* as love.

If the gesture you have been making is not being interpreted as a friendly act, perhaps you should reconsider its form. You may not have sensed your partner's lack of readiness for what you are about to do. Our habit is to say what we would like said and to consider this reasonable. However, if we truly wish to treat others as we ourselves would be treated, we must learn to take an honest reading of the other person before we act.

Except possibly when dealing with strangers, it is not accurate to claim that we don't know other people's egos well enough to predict what they will receive happily. In an argument we clearly know them well enough to say what will hurt or anger them.

The long warfares that Gayle and I waged in the early years of our marriage—which are funny to look back on but were highly separating at the time—have been put behind us for many years now, and we are working hard to progress beyond the smaller flare-ups that still occasionally occur. This is a reasonable goal, and the love between us grows with each little gain made. However, the resistance to changing from misusing to using our knowledge of our partner can be surprisingly deep. There were many times over a period of several years when I thought the task was proving impossible. Now I realize that it was not the task but my conflict over the ultimate goal that was holding me back.

Giving In

Consisting of impressions of our past, our ego was formed mostly in childhood and has been fortified ever since. It is a collection of conflicting lessons and beliefs that constitutes a self-image that does not match what we feel on the deeper levels of our mind or heart. We are not our ego, even though we each have one, carry it around with us at all times, and are influenced by it continually.

As we turn to our peaceful core, we come to realize that we do not believe this superficial nonsense we have been thinking for all these years. When this point is reached, the mind begins shedding its ego identity at a fairly steady rate. As it begins to melt away, we become increasingly capable of uniting with other people on their heart level.

We have in effect two identities, one that can join and one that cannot. As long as we defend our ego, our imaginary identity, we feel a strong resistance to giving in to a union of two hearts because we recognize that our sense of autonomy or separateness will be weakened in the process.

Nothing we truly want can be lost by loving too much. This fear, this resistance to giving in, only protects our unhappiness. If for just an instant we could see how utterly unimportant are these stands we are always taking, these opinions that must be respected, these personality traits that must be justified, we would know that sacrifice is never what is being asked of us. You do not want what you fight for—you want what you betray in order to fight.

What could you possibly lose by seeking the peace of another person—by literally making another's peace your single-minded goal? You can certainly lose by destroying another's peace. In fact, loss will be the one reliable outcome each time you must be right. You can certainly lose by loving too little. But to love too much is to dare to be yourself, to be your own heart, which is all you have ever wanted to be.

In the West especially, many have assumed that the way to have a more reliable life and a more consistent state of mind is to "get tough." One must not for a minute let up on one's body, one's behavior, or even on one's children and employees. Throughout America teenagers are pursued through the house by irate parents yelling, "Once again you didn't take out the garbage." Young people see the painful lives of their elders and believe they can avoid their aching loneliness by learning to keep their distance: "If it's inevitable I will suffer little desertions all my life, I must avoid getting close enough to anyone for it to hurt."

The unexamined assumption is that our pain comes from closeness and gentleness. Thus parents assume that incessant scolding and other forms of "parental distance" result in better control of their two-year-old or that pushing their own body past its limits will eventually hush its little ways of whining. The thought of showing their body constant compassion seems as unreasonable to most people as being a true friend to their child or viewing strangers as their brothers and sisters.

The pain of betrayal, faithlessness, and mockery enters through the ego, not the heart. Hardness, bitterness, withdrawal, anger, and other compassionless qualities that are turned to as means to steel ourselves against the falling away of friends and loved ones make the mind more vulnerable to suffering rather than less.

You will never suffer by being too faithful to another. If you do suffer it will not be from love. The common counsel that the risk we must take if we want to draw closer to another person is the pain of rejection is as impractical a piece of advice as it is false in its supposition that love can convey us to loneliness or that light can bring us the dark. There are definite causes of suffering, but gentleness, kindness, and acceptance are not among them.

The Ego Alliance

Although egos cannot unite, they can form alliances, and most relationships are no more than this. The nature of this foundation makes them eminently vulnerable to fallings-out and breakups. They are also increasingly unhappy because there is always a growing dynamic of separation present. This is found within relationships of all forms—between lovers, children and parents, acquaintances, and of course within marriages—and essentially it is the feeling of "you and me against the world."

Within such an alliance there may be a strong accord between the parties, especially on what is wrong with everyone else. A community of like interests is discovered or formed that generates on both sides an impression of agreement and closeness, yet when it is examined more carefully it can be seen that these links are not so much mutual loves as similar dislikes. The ego part of us is never wholly certain of what it likes. Yet it feels more definite about its dislikes.

The basis of the average relationship is a mutuality of targets: the reprehensible conduct of the government and which candidate is "loved" for saying it like it is. The destructive policy of schools and which authorities are recommended because they agree. The movies that are poorly done and which are the temporary favorites. And especially the behavior on the part of certain individuals that is laughable or objectionable and what contrasting behavior on the part of other individuals that is just wonderful.

There is no true love and acceptance in any of this. What makes this foundation of a family's bond, of two couples' enthusiasm for each other, of a crew's spirit, of a friendship's fidelity, so tenuous is that fear and anger are self-immolating. Judgment cannot be felt for anyone outside of a relationship without also being felt within it. Therefore relationships that are mere alliances are ultimately destructive of the participants' happiness.

Several summers ago the four of us took a trip to the San Juan Islands. We rented a small American-built station wagon at the airport and transported it to Orcas Island on one of the large ferryboats that shuttles there. In Santa Fe we lived on a long rough dirt road, and we had to switch to foreign-built cars because the various domestic ones we tried were demolished usually within a few months of purchasing them. Without being aware of it, we had developed a prejudice against all American vehicles.

We were three days into our vacation before Gayle and I realized why the tone between the four of us was not good. It seemed that every few hours something new would fall off the station wagon, and all the time we had been driving it we had kept up a running commentary. One day Gayle was outside a grocery store when a man came up and asked how she liked her new wagon. "It's a terrible, terrible car," she said, and delivered our by now well-practiced list of horrors. "Oh," he said sadly, "I just bought one." Gayle is a very kind person and she backtracked as fast as she could, blaming the rental agency, retrograde planets, and everything else she could think of and told the man she was certain he had not made a mistake, that it was actually a fine car. And of course he didn't believe a word of it.

Once we realized that our critical frame of mind would not stay put—even though the target was inanimate—we surrounded the station wagon in light, resolved to think of it gently, and as an inevitable result the happiness we felt being together increased. Quite naturally this also spilled over onto John and Jordan—but not onto the wagon, which remained as problematic as ever, thus giving us lots of grist for the mill.

Gayle and I had long since recognized that it destroyed our gentleness toward each other for us to indulge in judging other people, but we had not seen that to merely deplore the car one is driving, the house one is renting, the city where one is living puts the relationship back on an alliance-of-hate basis and wipes out the quite fragile flow of loving feelings. Of course, many couples have not yet had a period of peace long enough for its absence to be noticed. Yet once a real relationship begins to form, the rewards are so substantial that the amount of work required to keep it growing is usually eagerly and happily given. This is why it is so important for couples to have hope. A real relationship is an attainable goal! And it provides the most powerful sanctuary from the chaos and pain of the world. This is so because when two hearts unite, when two who were separate become one, no matter how they choose to describe it, they experience what has been called the Divine; they experience Home.

CHAPTER 17

Loved Ones

What Is a Real Relationship?

The great and fatal wound of humanity is the ancient belief that selfishness works. What we have before us now is just a new version of a very old sadness. The true need—as it has always been—is merely to love, to accept, to be quick to help, to be slow to judge. And the reason is simple. You *are* forgiving and kind at heart. The one trait you will never be able to change is your gentleness. On the level where it exists, you are united with, not at odds with, the interests of every living thing. This truth gives you enormous potential for forming real relationships.

What then is a love-based or heart-based relationship? Who are the "loved ones" we all speak of?

The dominant feeling in a real relationship is "you and me for the world"—the precise opposite of the alliance-based relationship's "you and me against the world." Upon first glance this may seem an unattainable and silly position. Yet far more effort is required to misunderstand others than simply to let them be. By trying to cast most individuals outside their relationship as different or dangerous, a couple or a family puts their own relationship under great tension and drives a wedge of guilt between themselves. It is never feasible to permanently unite *against*, because love is the only uniting force that endures.

However, it is possible to take the impulses of acceptance and gentleness and try to turn them into rules of behavior. Being gentle doesn't mean becoming a doormat. And accepting others doesn't mean joining them in their selfish or hurtful acts. Love says "No" as effortlessly as it says "Yes." It seeks far more than to be inoffensive. Love is kind even to another's ego but never cowers before it. Instinctively the love in you will side with the goodness of the other person, but the other person may not respond positively. There is, after all, free will.

One common confusion that results from turning love into rules occurs when a relative or intimate friend makes a difficult request. Our mind begins to shuttle between the experience of love and our picture of what love is supposed to look like, and we become conflicted.

How can we know if a request comes from another person's ego? Our happiness never entails judging anyone, and so we don't have to concern ourselves with where a request comes from but merely with its effect on our mind. Any request that calls to our fear should be looked at carefully.

You will often have a sinking feeling or a tinge of guilt just before you start to acquiesce to a demand that will hurt you. Just as with any question that comes into your mind, practice looking at the fears it generates and not at the question itself. When our mind is focused on a question, it is not focused on the answer. The answer is our state of mind. When the mind becomes preoccupied with a question, it gets noisy and scattered. Since the mind is our source of quiet knowing, our function is to keep it quiet.

Although there is no general recognition of this, gentleness is in fact firmness because gentleness is reliable and trustworthy. But within the general culture, anger, irritation, and moodiness are considered forms of firmness or toughness. Yet these emotions produce weakness and volatility. For instance, way too many parents discipline out of their mood. Because they are unpredictable, they merely end up making their children afraid of them. One night the child is ignored or thought funny for kicking the parent while being dressed for bed. On another night the child is snapped at or worse for the same behavior. This approach increases resentment, even in young children, and can end up making them as erratic as their parents.

Parents who are deeply gentle refuse to react out of their passing moods and are therefore consistently in a position to steer the child away from the unhappy approaches to life that any youngster is sure to try out from time to time.

Acceptance is frequently seen as a dangerous concept, and it obviously runs counter to the values of our times. Unfortunately, these values are particularly hostile to the formation of real relationships. We know a mom and dad who have a nine-year-old who loves outer space cartoons. They regularly tape those they feel are not too disturbing and let her watch them after school, but they allow no TV during meals and certain other times of day. A few years ago the couple took in the husband's elderly father, who is mentally sound and relatively healthy but no longer has the stamina to live alone. For over a year feelings between the father and the son were stirred up daily by the son's insistence that his father's longstanding habit of watching TV during dinner could not be permitted in their household.

In the course of receiving counseling, the son discovered that he was the victim of an almost universal attitude within relationships: He could not give in because he had already lost too much ground. In this case to his wife, to his daughter, and in years past, to his father. Once he recognized the meaninglessness of this "fact," he was able to open his eyes to the many options he had to resolve the issue. The one he chose was to buy another TV and invite his father to watch his programs and take whatever meals he wished in his bedroom. His daughter did not object to unequal treatment as he had feared; in fact, she was relieved at the improvement in atmosphere.

The aggrieved feeling of always losing ground, of always having to be the one who compromises, is a much encouraged attitude of our time. Many articles, talk shows, interviews with celebrities, and self-help books feed the current wisdom that one's personal "growth" comes before all else. Above all we need our space, our energy, our time. Every individual has a right to sex at a certain level of excitement, to a job that fulfills, to a partner and children who know just when to leave us alone. This is what you have coming, and you must not back down on any of it. The many pronouncements on this subject can sound virtuous, practical, and even mystically or spiritually grounded, and we have all perhaps been unconsciously influenced by them to some degree.

What then must we do to join rather than ally ourselves with another? First we must look inside and see there someone who knows peace, someone who knows genuine love. We must feel the existence of such a self somewhere within, no matter how layered over. Then we must be willing to step beyond our egos, beyond our scared little defensive identity, and into that person we wish to be—one who does not look for faults, one who is not temperamental, one who is not jealous. And we must be willing to do this a hundred times a day if necessary. This may seem terribly, impossibly beyond our abilities. And so we simply begin.

Meeting the Like-Minded

The makings of your first real relationships are before you now. They are already within the bounds of your present daily routine. Two friends, an individual and an animal, an adult child and an elderly parent—there is no end to the many potentially tender and lovely relationships available, if only a start is made and the effort continued as best you can.

But remember that the effort is to see innocence and is not a flurry of smothering gestures. It is to think gently and *not* to get a gentle response. It is to give peace and not to be "left in peace." It is to understand even when misunderstood. If for example you are a father and you are estranged from your adult son, your function is to be a loving dad. It is not to have a loving son. If you are a mother and your daughter doesn't respect your opinions, your function is to respect hers. Concentrating on doing our part is actually a simpler approach to life than watching to see if others are doing theirs. Much simpler.

As you put yourself in a mental position to have real relationships, they begin occurring naturally—provided you aren't too picky. It is not wise to target a specific person and place your hopes on this one individual's reaction. If you will in a sense make yourself one-half of a real relationship, other halves will blossom around you. But, again, avoid anticipating changes in individual people, otherwise you will build up your expectations and become increasingly self-absorbed.

It's important that you rule out no one with whom you have contact, unless it's a person who calls to the worst in you. Just practice being a friend to the person before you now and you will gradually discover those who are capable of connection.

Even though the world puts great value in numbers, you don't wish to count your friends like a miser counts money. Be rich in your ability to stay at peace. Be the kind of person you want to be, and because of the nature of the human heart, you will see the like-minded.

Since it's the repeated small beginnings and not the grand breakthroughs that carry us forward, I want to suggest a limited but effective way of practicing being a person who is capable of real relationship.

- Select one or two events where you will be encountering a few people over a sustained period, such as a party, a visit with your parents, an outing with a friend. As close to the beginning of each occasion as feasible, schedule a brief period of mental preparation. Five or 10 minutes should do.

- During this time decide how you wish to be on this occasion. Do you want to be strong? Kind? Peaceful? Centered? Select whatever qualities epitomize your heart's desire. Don't pick behaviors that run counter to your usual personality. For instance, if you are usually reticent, don't decide to be witty. Choose an inner atmosphere, not an affectation.

- Take the upcoming occasion into your mind and imagine your being this kind of person within it. Start at the beginning, perhaps your arrival at the place, and picture your every response coming from your chosen mindset. Remember that you alone are the focus of this exercise. Therefore imagine people and events as they will probably be and not as you would like them. Go through the occasion in detail. Fantasize any range of expected or unexpected occurrences, but see your whole, consistent self remaining the same. Be very disciplined about this, picturing each happening carefully until you have seen yourself through the entire event.

- During the event itself, let yourself be. If at some point you realize that you have forgotten your purpose, take a break (go to the car, into the rest room, ask to use the phone) and gently remind yourself of it. Then return to the occasion and relax into what is going on. Do not anxiously monitor yourself. Your preparation before the event was like giving your boat a shove into the water. So now just row merrily.

Choose Your Encounters Gently

It would be possible to have a relationship with almost anyone if we could somehow refrain from seeking signs of reciprocity. If we would not place our hope in another's ego, we could perhaps sense more easily the person's true feelings and would experience a kinship with this individual, whatever form that might take. Even though this is always a potential, often it's not helpful to have frequent contact with everyone available. Egos never love, but they do relate less disturbingly with some people than with others.

Although mandatory relationships in the workplace are an exception, how much another's personality clashes with yours needs to be considered. If you see that you simply can't be around some individual without it upsetting you, there are other ways of practicing love besides direct contact. Perhaps a complete break is not necessary, but if you need to step back, that action does not have be defined as irrevocable.

Never abandon anyone in your heart, and if your actions symbolize rejection, refuse to give them this interpretation yourself. Whenever you step back with your body, step forward with your mind. Maintain within you a place of tolerance for the person, and don't confuse yourself by thinking that you must discard your peace because of the appearance your withdrawal presents. Your ego will argue this, but continuing to love is your right.

Do not insist on relating in only one way to someone who is difficult for you. Whenever feasible, don't put yourself in circumstances where you are likely to make more mistakes than usual. You subject yourself to discouragement when your mistakes come too closely together. If situations that are hard for you go on too long, your reserves of peace become depleted and you begin losing ground. Sometime, of course, this can't be avoided.

Naturally there are relationships, such as with family members, that must be maintained in some way, because to turn completely from one's adult child or elderly parent can be more disturbing to one's mental health than occasional contact. However, the difficulty of these encounters can often be modified. A mother may discover that she is lectured less by her son through e-mail than on the phone. A father may use formula to feed the baby on periodic nights in order to give his wife a needed break from the baby. A sister may find that her brother is less argumentative if the visits take place at his house. We have a friend who phones his mother only during the day because the cocktails she has after dinner always make her maudlin and manipulative. Our ego is reluctant to take the simple step that will make a difference. The battle must be fought out on the same grounds until it is won—but in relationships there are no triumphs.

Within a difficult relationship it is also helpful to understand our role in maintaining the problem. Often we set ourselves up for disappointment and pain by continuing to act in ways that have created friction in the past. We play out the role that has been given us, particularly in long-term relationships, and so we say and do what is expected of us. When another calls us to respond as we always have, it is always possible not to answer the call.

Don't Be Too Spiritual at Work

Many of us have relationship problems in the workplace. We find that disturbing encounters or disturbing atmospheres are the norm. Putting many people together under the same roof, as is necessary in some businesses, creates a rolling sea of anxieties, jealousies, sexual tensions, depressions, expectations, and competitions. Along with persistent moods, there are passing thoughts and feelings all around us, and often as the day goes on the effect is tiring and confusing. Naturally this makes it difficult to practice some of the things we have been discussing, especially when the boss, a supervisor, or certain coworkers are truly disturbing.

Often the best approach is not to try to practice any philosophy at all but to simply go to work and do the job like a cog in a machine. The feeling is somewhat like leaving one set of clothes outside the workplace and putting on a separate set for the job. In this sense, the object is to practice shutting down our awareness so as not to pick up all the thoughts and emotions that swirl around us. As you drive or commute to work, slowly become this cog.

By no means does this require us to do a sloppy job. In fact it offers us a measure of insulation if we stay in the present, do the best job we can, and be thoughtful and kind to the people around us. So it is an excellent, not a shoddy, set of work clothes we put on. We are a celestial cog!

Gossip is a staple of most workplaces, and generally speaking you will be happier if you don't resist this. There is no need to join in malicious gossip, no need to poison and be poisoned, no need to join an unkind alliance against a weak, misunderstood, or unfortunate individual. But very often the kind of gossip that one encounters at work is harmless and can even be fun.

Words are generally not the problem. If our heart is in a good place, we can usually let our mouth do whatever it does, just as we let our hands, feet, and eyes drive the car without trying to decide and control every movement.

The Gentle Option

The relationships one has should rest gently in the mind, cradled there like little flowers. They should refresh and brighten one's life. Truly there is no need for any association to torture us and to go on as a plague upon our life year after year. Yet so many commonplace encounters are no longer thought of sanely—the grown child and elderly parent, the couple of many years, the parent and adolescent, the terrible twos, the terrible in-laws.

It is believed that these and various other interrelations must be endured with some degree of unhappiness. There is even a certain pride taken in the sacrifice everyone "knows" is inherent. Jokes are made and sympathy given as if no option other than misery could possibly exist within these classic situations.

The older couple, the parent and child, and all the rest must not allow their minds to fall into these traps of dark categorization. If they do, they will find themselves playing out a needless tragedy with no insight as to a way out. It's not that there are no inherent difficulties in these situations, for of course there are, but no implacable law of unhappiness is at work within any relationship, no matter what stage it has entered. Those involved should not only free themselves of preconceptions, but they should also be wholly open to options of any sort. Take for example an evening at home.

Feeling at Home

If all our individual prejudices were gathered together, probably no aspect of any relationship would escape some degree of self-fulfilling dread. We have discussed how on one hand the world looks to relationships for solutions to all its problems and how on the other hand it sets up various ordinary interactions to be inescapable little hells. A time of relating that should be quite happy, according to the lip service accorded it, is the evening of the day. One is now off work, household chores are finished, and there is nothing to do but enjoy one's spouse or child or pet or all of the above. Some people believe so completely in this fiction that they actually commit suicide if they don't have it. They think they have been uniquely cursed because their life never offered it to them.

After sitting in schoolrooms much of the day, or in front of the TV, younger kids often have a store of energy that they haven't released, and come evening they are ready to play. Their idea of fun usually involves acting out their imaginations in some energetic and repetitious way. Adults on the other hand are usually tired and slightly discouraged by the end of the day, and their idea of fun is often some quiet activity like reading, talking with friends, eating leisurely, or watching TV. And so the prevailing evening state in most families is a continuous, though perhaps covert, battle of wills. The adults feel constantly interrupted and the children feel neglected, and of course both are correct. Once again, there are always many ways around any unhappy dynamic, but they require openness to options and some initial effort.

The happiness of the family rests in its attempts to join

rather than to withdraw into private pleasures. This does not mean that everyone must stay in the same room doing the same thing or that adults must give up their TV or evening newspaper. It means only that the mind itself does not exclude or long for some show of togetherness to be over with so that one can again be self-devoted.

The ego does not understand that minds can continue touching even while bodies are separately engaged. Thus the principle is the same. Do not indulge in idle feelings of judgment or fear. Keep thought gentle. Keep the mind soft. Think kindly and easily rather than rigidly and unhappily. And put your mental arms around those who are not beside you. Much less work is required to spend the evening this way than in defensive withdrawal. Just watch and try, watch and try, and your gain will be gradual . . . and immense.

As to what specifically a family can do to begin eliminating the customary evening strain, perhaps a small amount of time could be set aside to try different activities. If the children of the family are young, maybe just before sleep everyone could join in letting go of the day. As children get older, there are an increasing number of games that can be played, and often just a few minutes spent this way can brighten the atmosphere remarkably. As an example, a game might be played in which the entire family sits in a circle and takes each individual in turn and surrounds that person in light and sees them as wonderful and just perfect as is. Of course children frequently have to be helped with these things and gently shown, and you must remember that they may act silly, because acting silly is part of their idea of fun.

In a variation of this, a clock or timer might be used, the alarm set, and when it rings everyone switches to the next person. And so you begin with the individual on your right, surround that person in light, and at the sound of the alarm go to the second person on your right, and so on around the circle. In this way everyone is being surrounded in light by someone at all times. A little game like this can be very nice.

In another version, perhaps something is done verbally. Mother begins and says, "Daddy is friendly. Daddy is silly. Daddy is nice." And each one in turn adds some kind points about Daddy. Then this is done with the next family member, and the next, always keeping the remarks gentle. Very soon a sense of joining and oneness has been created.

A family might also do playful activities such as "Time In," during which the child can speak openly, perhaps even an entire evening of silly talk. Children love this—just silly, crazy talk. Or songs that each one adds to the lyrics. Or funny sounds or funny faces that everyone tries to guess. Parents frequently think they cannot be silly and still maintain discipline, but that is silly. Yet silliness may not feel natural to some parents, and to force a person into this role would defeat the purpose of joining.

Parents must learn not to make decisions out of fear of the future but to make them in the present interests of their family. The games that are played should be ones that strengthen love, strengthen the bond, and that increase the family's real treasure, which is the affection they have for each other.

Because music bypasses words, it can also bring people together. I have seen the unhappy atmosphere of a car ride quickly change when a Raffi tape was played. And one does not have to be proficient to play musical instruments oneself. If your purpose is love and not a conflicted sense of first having to meet some unclear standard, you can have great fun with a kazoo, harmonica, drum, or just blowing into bottles. There is also drawing, painting, sculpting, and a hundred other arts and disciplines.

The aim of all these activities is simplicity and happiness, not artistic invention. So many of us are afraid of trying our own ideas because we don't believe they are "creative enough." We carry with us a hampering mental image of how the activity should look, and we either do nothing or do it in conflict. It is always better to try than to remain stymied because of fear.

As children age they usually have homework and other activities that occupy much of their time, and it is important to recognize and respect this rather than insisting that togetherness must continue to look the same. Needs change, and flexibility and understanding are crucial.

In All Things Hope and Try, Try and Hope

If all our relationships—the chance encounter, the short-term, the lifelong—could somehow be stripped of both dread and anticipation, and if we could look at other people as opportunities to be at peace, as chances to relax and see innocently, then this anciently agitated aspect of the world could recede into the ordinary and once again be a normal and happy part of life. There is no real reason why this can't occur. All it requires on our part is awareness, awareness of how we make the mistakes in the first place, of how we set ourselves up for pain through our expectations and see them through with our need to be right.

Once we begin recognizing the attitudes and approaches that undermine any chance we have of being at peace while in the presence of another body, we will naturally and effortlessly discard them. Thus it is so very important that we remain hopeful and encouraged. Relationships don't have to be a whirlwind that constantly lifts us up and casts us down. Yet we have gotten ourselves into some unfortunate mental habits that are preventing remedy. Therefore work hard, for it is happy work. Do not lie down before the world's insanity on the subject of relationship. Do not be trampled by your passing moods and tiny emotions. A deep serenity is still attainable. Immerse yourself in gentleness. The world cannot withstand your love.

CHAPTER 18

WRAP-UP

Happiness is not noisy. It is not a special time set aside, a party, a "happy hour," an event that stands out above other events. Happiness is not even a thing to do. It may be possible to schedule excitement, but it's not possible to schedule genuine happiness. As we have all seen, pre-planned forays into fun sometimes end up making real happiness more difficult to come by.

Happiness is not some fantasy that comes from a song or a movie. Because of its harmlessness, happiness is incapable of favoritism. Nor is it a state that can be compared. It is not enough to know that there are those who suffer more than we do. Happiness is not in the jungle but in the clear, quiet stream that runs through it. We need neither wits, nor cleverness, nor insensitivity, nor anger to get "our share" of it. In fact, we need very little.

If you adhere to the handful of principles discussed in this book, you will unquestionably come to know a reliable and growing happiness. There is not a great deal to learn. Your attainment rests far more in your readiness to make an effort than in the elegance of your approach. Although the world believes that mistakes have great importance and should be recalled and mulled over for significance and guilt, and must definitely be used to hammer oneself into a better person, the truth is that mistakes are not important. Starting over is important. A faulty approach must first be recognized, then discarded. When we continue dwelling on weakness, we are not practicing strength.

The components of happiness are quite simple. Happiness is gentleness, peace, concentration, simplicity, forgiveness, humor, fearlessness, trust, and now. In its true form each quality includes all the rest, for happiness is whole, and one feels whole when genuinely happy.

Simplicity

Simplicity is a characteristic that can't be judged by appearances. It is a stability, a settledness, a straightforwardness, a purity of the mind that is often expressed in a simpler lifestyle—a simpler diet, a more orderly routine, a more intelligent use of time, less clutter, less financial chaos, fewer involvements—in other words, less world, more peace. These are common effects, but there are no rules, no strictures, no external measurements of one's mastery of simplicity.

It is possible to be quite wealthy and still be simple. One's house may be larger than ordinary, one's business activities more widespread. Likewise, one can own nothing and do little and be thoroughly mixed up and disjoined. Simplicity can find pleasure in unexpected and overlooked places, such as one's family and job. Let's say you are a man and that you hold the ordinary male-ego position of believing that somehow you should not be saddled with child care. Your wife, say, is sick, and suddenly you find yourself alone with the baby. Being a man, you immediately engage in a project that's not necessary *at that moment*. Whereas if you pause, your heart will counsel you to drop everything and concentrate on the essential—caring for your child. Seeing this, perhaps you plop down in a chair and just hold the baby. And if that makes you happy, and the baby happy, it is enough.

For most people, preparing for bed and getting ready in the morning are difficult times, yet they will entertain almost any idea that could add further complications. Whether it is one of those times or some other recurring distress, remember that happiness is always a possibility. During your moments of difficulty help yourself by doing less, by thinking less, by relating gently, by being one thing. Leave the world undisturbed. Simply be simple. There is nothing more to happiness than this.

Now

It's as if a cult has formed around the concept of "being present," "being centered," "being mindful." Those who do not speak in present-tense terms or eschew gathering nuts for the winter are considered spiritually backward.

Allowing one's mind to be at ease now instead of later never entails self-conscious mannerisms or a practiced vocabulary. It certainly doesn't imply that we should not provide for our future needs or those of our family. The universe does not reward you with money because you have the right beliefs. So don't quit your job, cancel your insurance, or let bills slip in the name of trusting the present. All this will do is make you needlessly anxious and can even result in your abandoning in disgust a gentle approach to life.

Possibly the primary mistake we make that keeps us from the present is that we expect too much of a memory or an anticipation. We can offer ourselves little more than tension when we pursue a time that is absent. The present is not somehow more virtuous. It's just that this instant is the only time we have the opportunity to be happy. So why waste it?

We can't have fun thinking outside the present without our reveries soon deteriorating. These thoughts have meaning only as comparisons and must always continue into their opposites. The mind can't be controlled when off in unreal realms. No way exists to be happy this afternoon, this evening, after the divorce, after finals, after the loan goes through. The mind can never fool itself for very long that the uncertain is certain. It constantly revises its version of later in a sad attempt to arrive at one that will come to rest and satisfy. There is no real harm in this, but the present has more potential.

No better time exists than now, and the hope that there might be a better time has cost us many opportunities to be happy. Let the present remain with you and spread out its calm blanket of acceptance at your feet. In the present you are free. Leave behind all that is behind, and know the lightness, the happiness that practicing the present can bring.

Never make the mistake of fighting to stay in the present. There is no code of thoughts to think. If your mind feels restricted and rigid, it is not practicing happiness. So allow the day to come to you. Let each event arrive in its own time. Do not try to override the moment, to judge the moment, and somehow get beyond it. Now is no more than an absence of fear.

The *literal* content of the ideas we think must always involve some aspect of the future or past. Remaining in the present means staying within a circle of peace, not thinking present tense thoughts. We simply think from peace and from ease. We don't make silly rules about good and bad subjects. Tension is the clue that our heart has shifted, that we are no longer interested in thinking in a peaceful way. What other time but now can touch the heart and bring rest to the mind? When else is there the chance to forgive and join another in love? Be where you are. Love the ones you are with. Enjoy the moment you are given. Bless the life you have. There is nothing more to happiness than this.

Gentleness

Gentleness is not a physical protector. It is a mode of thinking. Only the mind can poison the day. The day can't poison the mind. A truly gentle mind will remain happy under even difficult circumstances. But if gentleness is interpreted as meaning that we have created an atmosphere in which we are immune to being hurt, this is not gentleness but self-delusion. What logic is there in going into a rough neighborhood to demonstrate that we are gentle? Nor does practicing gentleness imply that we should continue in a situation in which we are being cheated or that we should finish going through our shopping list in a store whose employees are mean-spirited.

If we value our state of mind, we take the necessary steps to protect it. Obviously this doesn't include saying things that are likely to be misunderstood or doing what will be taken the wrong way. The reason we frequently do more harm than good is that we have not stopped to see what the other person actually wants. Gentle people are also thoughtful of themselves and do not make offers that are unnecessary.

Gentleness can take up any subject without harming it, without wishing it harm. It sees no harm in a face, a word, a mannerism, a stance, an opinion. It does not condemn weakness or fear anger. It neither hides from the world nor kicks against it. It is adaptable, it makes allowances, it understands, it has nothing to prove. Thus it remains itself. And there is nothing more to happiness than this.

Peace

Peace, or freedom from conflict, is the core of happiness. In learning to watch our sense of peace we avoid unhappiness. All forms of misery are heralded by a frame of mind that must become immediately recognizable if we are to gain mastery in happiness. If you are not clear about what you are getting ready to do or say, you are on the verge of scattering your thoughts and throwing away your peace. Mental conflict is not all that hard to recognize, we are just grossly out of practice.

Peace is the willingness not to rush. You can always tell an ego impulse by the little sense of urgency you will feel: "Do it quickly before it's too late." Too late for what? In your rush to be unhappy, notice how vague and confused you are about the reasons for not pausing and becoming clear. "Hurry or there will be consequences." But what consequences? Do not be afraid to stop and examine this argument. Our scared little ego places great value on not wasting time, on being fast, on the quick opinion, the immediate retort. So remind yourself that a moment's stopping is not a waste. Practice being slow—slow to react, slow to anger, slow to judge, slow to have an opinion.

Appearances are not as important as our mind. We wouldn't think of leaving the house with our hair and clothes in disarray, yet we are quite consistent in disregarding our mental state. We believe that only what can be seen has value, and since our thoughts are out of sight they signify very little. Provided our life appears well ordered, they may ramble in any direction, and so long as they remain hidden from others, they can do us no harm. This is a core belief around which unhappiness spins. We can't repeat the following idea too often: Appearances don't matter, only my mind matters. For if our mind is in a state of peace, we will deal with appearances quite well.

Take the time to look in your heart and be clear. Practice

doing each thing in peace. Walk through life being whole. Make your mind your clear, whole, peaceful home. Do not be afraid to admit to yourself how important your mind is to you, and do not be afraid to act this out by pausing as often as needed. The time has come to be very direct. Do you want to be happy? Then you want to have peace. There is nothing more to happiness than this.

Forgiveness

Anger and judgment can sometimes poison circumstances instantly, sometimes slowly, but whether their first effects are "controlled" or "unrepressed," they are never wholly eliminated from the system through some alchemy of time. In fact, people tend to become more narrow and bitter the older they get. The buildup occurs because the validity of the judging "faculty" is never questioned. Grievances are swept into corners of the mind, and gradually there is no room to think, no room for light, no room for fun. Now each judgment becomes part of our identity, a point of pride, and we don't like having them questioned.

Forgiveness is the alternative, but forgiveness does not mean releasing all criminals from prison or spending more time with someone who pushes our buttons. Forgiveness is a thought, not a behavior. It is an inner expression of self-respect and integrity. The grounds for forgiving are simple: Grievances are unworthy of you.

As we go through the day, it's as if at some point we are shot with a poisoned arrow, and although not recognized at the time, the deterioration begins. Something happens, we interpret it, and this little picture, carried in the mind, begins releasing its toxins. Soon we are reacting badly to almost everything and we don't know why. It just seems that "things are not going well," even though on other occasions we have been able to glide through far more than this.

Form the habit of scanning your mind—not second-guessing your motives but staying aware of what your ego, your fear of happiness, is up to. The thoughts that arrest the mind must be recognized before the mind can be set free. Your own ego can become like the neighbor's dog you have agreed to take for a walk. Your function is to keep it moving along and not let it stop and sniff. When it gets too interested, it gets in trouble. And it is when your ego stops to dwell on some wrong, some unfairness, some slight, that you will feel injured.

How many remarks were inoffensive until we thought about them? How many mistakes failed to delay us until we turned them into sins?

To forgive means no more than to continue walking toward your goal. If you see that some picture of an earlier event is poisoning you, do not try to dishonestly change the picture, for you will think you are trying to alter reality. Merely look closely at it and let it go.

Forgive, but don't wonder how you must now act. Forgive, but don't try to convince another to forgive. Forgive, but don't hold yourself superior because you have done so. Simply forgive. Wrap your forgiveness around you like a cloak of light, an armor that protects your happiness but closes no one out. Forgiveness is not a "the devil can take you" attitude. It is a clear shield of love that lets the person in but does not let in judgments that betray the person.

The armor you wear is your goodwill. Put it on every day and the arrow of circumstance will not penetrate. This will be so because you will not send the arrow back. Nor will you take it with you. You will think nothing of it. And there is nothing more to happiness than this.

Humor

A laugh is the most beautiful sound on Earth. As it rings in one heart it resonates in others, and it always has the effect of helping people feel closer, feel understood and appreciated. It is like a little shower of love, a bubble of happiness that can't help popping. It rises out of peace, passes through an ease of manner, and bursts forth naturally. A gentle nature offers no resistance to humor because it sees innocence in the world and feels no need to hold back.

True humor is a continual welling up of happiness that very often children have. You can frequently see it just behind their eyes waiting for the flimsiest of excuses to overflow. When Jordan was three he made up jokes. He evidently thought that any sentence beginning with "Knock, knock" or "Why did _____ cross the road?" was bound to be funny. Although his jokes came out making no sense whatsoever, everyone laughed because he was so delighted and happy telling them.

Obviously humor is not merely stories, retorts, and being witty. And it is seldom found in kidding and questions. It can be pure and abundant without ever taking the conventional forms. The ego's version of humor requires that you understand what is *meant* and agree by laughing. And those who don't laugh are "humorless." Clearly, that is just another way of comparing and judging. True humor is not a mere sound in the throat. And it never shocks or jolts or makes people feel singled out and tense. Where is the fun in that?

Very often we lose our humor as the years pass and the problems mount. Our little jokes are increasingly based on separateness and are sophisticated and bitter. Where did the child go? It got lost in fear and seriousness. What the ego can't grasp is that happiness is not frivolous—happiness is serious.

Once we somehow knew not to let things become so real.

The world danced before us because we looked at it through dancing eyes. This is still possible. We are not going to change the world. And does anyone really want to be that arrogant? Isn't it enough to help those we *can* help?

Why do so many adults smile when a child—any child—walks into a room? Of course there are many who do not, but perhaps the ones who do have not completely forgotten a child's mind, the good, healthy way a child often feels and reacts. So be a little funny, a little relaxed, a little bit off guard. Sink back into your inherent pleasantness and gaze kindly at the world. The world is indeed a funny place. It is a Marx Brothers' movie in which nothing can go right. So kick off your shoes, tip back your chair, and enjoy the absurdity of it all. Become a little child. There is nothing more to happiness than this.

Fearlessness

Fear is one of the great depressors of happiness. The fearful part of our mind believes that happiness is a sign of weakness, and it is strongly drawn to every witness of this view. This is what, for example, creates the addictive quality of the news. We lust to know the worst of everyone, of every day. We feed on fear.

Certainly there is nothing sinister about articles on the famous, news briefs on crimes and disasters, or local stories about the winning streak of the local basketball team. Most reports, reviews, and even gossip columns are well meant, and many of these attempts to inform do no more harm than waste time.

But you cannot realistically expect your mind to function on a level higher than the level of ideas you continuously feed it. If you pepper your conversations with stories of fear and loss, if you memorize every negative statistic that comes your way, if you join every bandwagon against the newest bad guys, naturally you will be an anxious and depressed person, no matter how spicy a personality you contrive. *Of course* the world is a mess. Why does this fact require your constant vigilance?

In your heart you yearn to be at least a small answer to the world's great sadness, and you know that to do little more than dwell on other people's weaknesses is not fulfilling that yearning. A fearless mind heals because it gives hope. Without a word spoken or withheld, it encourages and calms. Certainly you lock up and buckle up and take your insurance umbrella—if those gestures help your mind to be less anxious. Unquestionably you take steps to protect your children, your pets, and the well-being of your own body. Fearlessness is not some silly pretense of being mystically immune to worldly dangers. It is uninterested in *appearing* fearless because it values so deeply the true state.

What I refer to in this book as our heart could also be called our deeper self, for that is how it feels—more fundamental, more collected, more rooted, more sure. Yet it slips into our chaotic mental courtroom without respectable credentials, for it refuses to promise results in worldly terms to substantiate its claim for a hearing. It merely whispers, "Do that thing you can do most peacefully. And do it easily and happily."

Notice how our minds have been trained to reject such simple-minded advice. Where are the endless questions of duty and responsibility? Where are the thousand clashing lessons from the past? Perhaps, for just a moment, we know the thing we could do most peacefully, but what can we recall that shows this particular course of action rewarding? And what can we anticipate that makes it safe? Very possibly, nothing at all. So what will we trust?

It is a good thing to begin noticing the gentle intrusion of "I want to" into the usual merry-go-round of "I really wonder if I should because this could happen if I do, yet if I don't there just might be this other consequence that would be worse." Rather than try to answer the impossible question "What will result?" and choosing a course that merely avoids our greatest fear, we have the alternative of doing what we want to do. There is no anxiety in "I want to," provided the desire is seen in peace, comes from peace, and is acted on in peace. Therefore walk gently and walk in peace. Step into yourself and walk without fear. There is nothing more to happiness than this.

Concentration

What we look at is what we experience. In the world we always gaze upon our quality of mind projected out. With every thought we are either judgmental or happy. Each thought is a focus, and it sees a world bathed in darkness or light. Of course for most of us, concentration is already so shattered that much of the day is a blur of gray and holds little meaning.

When John was four, I took him and his friend Luke into a cave near our house in Patagonia, Arizona. Neither of them thought the mice scurrying on the walls of particular interest. I found them rather cute, with their big ears and fuzzy winter coats, but was hurried along to other things. When I passed up a sort of smelly, sticky mineral goo that was oozing from the wall, the boys stopped and poked and sniffed and animatedly discussed its meaning. They did not consult me.

Whose judgment was correct? Which is better, little and cute or smelly and sticky? We look at thoughts, not at things. The most we can say is that we are true to our personal past. Yet is that all there is to be true to? The way "bloviators" on TV argue over what is a big or minor event, you would think the answer was "Yes."

There is a level of concentration that is outside of our individual histories. It is found in our ability to see with and through happiness. Happiness is always a possibility because the part of the mind that sees happily is capable of acceptance. And happiness that endures is also possible because the mind can decide to see this way permanently.

However, "seeing no evil" is not concentration since the decision of what is evil goes unquestioned. I know a man who used to turn his eyes to the other side of the street, or cross over, when he saw an attractive woman approaching. Maybe such a practice could simplify life for someone, but in his case it was done purely out of fear. Yet who can help noticing what the world marks as beautiful, or ugly, or horrible, or any other quality it teaches is worthy of attention? Concentration is not "putting on blinders." Rather, we notice in a new way. We notice from our happiness.

You can behold gentleness and peace and innocence in the world provided you understand that they come from you. A way must be found to pour forth the beauty of the soul. When your gaze is on the present and your eyes laugh, you shine on the world you see and the light of your heart goes before you. This is possible because you are something more than a body.

Be single-minded, be purposeful, be focused. Know who you are and what you want. Formulate your purpose into words, etch it on your heart, repeat it in your mind, and above all, live it and see it. The truth is true. Happiness is better than misery. Therefore, concentrate on happiness. Decide "Today I will be happy" and it will be so. There is nothing more to happiness than this.

Trust

We take our bodies to nutritionists, our minds to therapists, our children to schools, and our relationships to magazines. We are so used to thinking that any possible good must come from an outside source that we don't consider the alternative: There is something within us that knows.

The ego takes self-trust and turns it into ego-trust. To honor this "self" we are called upon to respect our irritation and self-ishness, as if they were our essence. We *do* know the wisdom of our heart. We *have* felt it. It's just that you and I get confused so often. We are told to doubt, and we doubt.

This is why our inner self appears to need developing—an absurd concept when you consider it, that we must somehow become more ourselves. But it does feel that way. So let us proceed slowly but directly. Let us try ourselves out a little at a time, until we are finally found worthy in our own eyes.

Today, begin trusting your own sense of happiness, of what makes you happy and what does not. Let it spread to your diet, your clothes, your relationships, your spiritual yearnings. Let it infuse your spending and saving, your health and your habitat. Sit down often and know your own heart. There is clearly a lot of weeding out to do, so many silly assumptions about what is exciting and desirable that you and I have falsely believed. So if a little experimenting and culling are required, that is a small sacrifice indeed. All it implies is that we might make some mistakes. We will try something we thought we wanted only to uncover a more profound desire.

Let the roots of your knowing deepen and expand. Water them with your patience and your clear purpose. Where is the shame in admitting that we have not yet arrived? Let the world rant about its absolute rightness, then let us respectfully return to our heart for the quiet answer.

Let peace be your friend. Take its hand often. Yield to its soft nudges, its broad and gentle preferences. Only the peace of your own heart can be relied on as completely as this. Practice trusting, and you will have the grounds for trust. Practice yourself, and you will know a self that touches others in true helpfulness.

Practice your heart, and you will be happy. There is nothing more to happiness than this.

And so, with this little wrapping-up chapter, our conversation ends, but not our joint effort and our mutual goal. We walk together, as do all those who have laid strife aside and set their eyes on love. This is the other way to pass through the world. It requires no special concepts, no excluding vocabulary, no particular beliefs, only enough hope in the possibility of love and peace to pursue them in one's family, one's job, on the streets, in the stores. Just a little willingness to try to be the kind of person we want to be—one who takes others as they are, who helps when a way to help is clear, who sees innocence in mistakes.

Let us then journey together. The distance to the heart is short indeed. Where else could it be but where you are? It is your right to be happy. This is what you were made for. And if you will not resist, happiness will find a way to pour from your heart and fill your days. Simply keep a place within you where it is welcomed, and happiness will come and abide with you forever.

ABOUT THE AUTHOR

Hugh Prather is the author of fifteen books, including the best-selling *Notes to Myself; Spiritual Notes to Myself; Love and Courage; The Little Book of Letting Go; Spiritual Parenting;* and *I Will Never Leave You.* He lives with Gayle, his wife and co-author of thirty-seven years, in Tucson, Arizona, where he is a resident minister at St. Francis in the Foothills United Methodist Church. Prather is also the host of *The Hugh Prather Show* on Wisdom Radio and Sirius Satellite Radio. Hugh and Gayle have three sons and a dog that thinks she's a cat.

OTHER BOOKS BY HUGH PRATHER

Notes to Myself

Spiritual Notes to Myself

A Book for Couples

I Will Never Leave You

Notes to Each Other

Love and Courage

Spiritual Parenting

The Little Book of Letting Go

TO OUR READERS

Conari Press publishes books on topics ranging from spirituality, personal growth, and relationships to women's issues, parenting, and social issues. Our mission is to publish quality books that will make a difference in people's lives—how we feel about ourselves and how we relate to one another. We value integrity, compassion, and receptivity, both in the books we publish and in the way we do business.

As a member of the community, we donate our damaged books to nonprofit organizations, dedicate a portion of our proceeds from certain books to charitable causes, and continually look for new ways to use natural resources as wisely as possible.

Our readers are our most important resource, and we value your input, suggestions, and ideas about what you would like to see published. Please feel free to contact us, to request our latest book catalog, or to be added to our mailing list.

CONARI PRESS

An imprint of Red Wheel/Weiser, LLC

P.O. Box 612

York Beach, ME 03910-0612

800-423-7087

www.conari.com